Woman's Journey without Children

Anita L. Ferrell

Table of Contents

ABSTRACT

For many, bearing children is not a choice, it is considered the norm, a rite of passage. Despite this view, in the past two decades, there has been a substantial increase in the number of families without children, and the number of women who do not have children has doubled. While women who have chosen to be without children have increasingly gained acceptance in society, they continue to experience varying degrees of stigma. This research project reviewed the literature on the topic of women without children, and investigated the subjective experience of ten women who have decided to not have children. This study explored the decision process, particularly, how the participants arrived at the decision to not have children as well as the impact their choice had on their sense of self. The method used was a semi-structured interview, and data from these interviews was analyzed to identify themes that emerged from the participants' narratives. The findings of this study revealed that the choice to forego motherhood is complex and that several factors can impact one's decision, including others' opinions. Some of these factors included their background and experience of being a child as well as their role within their family. The participants made reference to the way their mothers identified with being a 'mom' and not wanting to identify as such. They expressed doubts about their ability to manage parenting and bringing a child into a dangerous world. Also of concern was the idea of meeting the demands of parenting, including the expense of raising children. Lastly, the participants identified health reasons as a factor, as well as the physical demands of pregnancy and childbirth.

CHAPTER ONE

INTRODUCTION

There has been a significant rise in the number of families without children over the past few decades. Many more women are now reaching the end of their childbearing years without giving birth. The number of women without children has doubled over the past 20 years (Gold, 2012). The ratio of non-mothers to mothers, ages 18 to 28 years, in the 1970s was one-to-ten whereas, more recently, the ratio has been one-to-five. Over the past decade, the number of women of childbearing age who have not had children has risen for all ethnic groups and most educational levels (Livingston & Cohn, 2010). White women are the most likely to not have children; however, the past decade has shown a rapid increase in Black, Latina, and Asian women who have also decided not to have children, which has narrowed this racial disparity. The rise in women and families without children is growing in other countries as well, such as Canada, Australia, Great Britain, Italy, Sweden, Panama, and Brazil, among a few others (Gold, 2012). Remaining without children represents a significant change in the modern family for married or coupled women.

In the past, much of the research about women who had not had children viewed this as a problem. The language of popular discourse used to describe non-mothers frequently included terms such as "infertility" or "childlessness," denoting an absence or deficiency perspective. Women were subject to implicit prejudice for not having children. In recent years, the term *childfree* has been used by those who regard this state as the product of an active and fulfilling choice. Though the terms "childfree" and "childless" are often used synonymously, "childfree" refers to people who intentionally choose not to bear or have children; whereas "childless" refers to individuals who desire

1

to have children but are unable to do so (Gold, 2012). This is an important distinction because, while there has been much research on women who are involuntarily childless, less attention has been paid to women who choose to be childfree.

Traditional normative cultural discourses on gender and feminine identity have tended to view participating in motherhood as a crucial achievement of women and a manifestation of the ideal identity of womanhood. Being a mother has traditionally been regarded as one of the most important decisions that a woman makes in her life (Brandalesi & Bernardi, 2013; Peterson & Engwall, 2013). Motherhood is often viewed as an essential component for feminine gender identity, optimal self-esteem, and well-being. Gillespie (2003) cogently describes motherhood as part of ideal femininity:

> … the nurturance of children has historically been seen to be what women *do*, and mothers have been seen to be what women *are*, constituting the central core of normal, healthy feminine identity, women's social role and ultimately the meanings of the term *woman* (p.225).

Women who do not express the desire to become mothers have been perceived with negative stereotypes, and have been viewed as selfish, vain, unwomanly, neurotic, or childhaters. They have been assumed to lead less fulfilling lives. Various theories have been offered to understand the basis for these negative and hostile attitudes. The literature indicates that there may be multiple factors mediating the stigmatization of women who choose not to have children, including deviation from traditional gender roles, ethnic values, and violation of religious imperatives (Gillespie, 2003; Mueller & Yoder, 1999; Vinson et al., 2010).

Despite the stereotypes and assumptions, some women have rejected the inextricable link between motherhood and womanhood. A growing, but limited body of research is accumulating that explores the choice to be childfree and the impact that decision has on self-esteem and life adjustment (Gillespie, 2003; Gold, 2012; Peterson &

Engwall, 2013). Research has shown that women have diverse reasons for making this

decision. For some, the decision seems to be pragmatic, including career orientation,

monetary advantages, and desire for more time with their significant other. Others

express reasons that are more philosophical or psychological, such as concerns about

world overpopulation, gender identity, gender role, or early childhood or childcare

experiences (Gillespie, 2003; Mollen, 2006).

Societal changes have made it more acceptable for women to openly voice their

choice to be without children. Of the existing studies that have explored this topic, most

studies of women who have chosen not to have children, have been gathered from

women who were in their early to mid-40s. These women were raised in the early phases

of the second wave of feminism beginning in the mid-1960s and 1970s. Since that time,

there has been considerable societal change in expectations around feminine gender

identity. As such, it is not clear how these changes have affected women, who were

raised after feminist notions became more culturally accepted, in relation to their

decisions regarding having children.

Gillespie (2003) proposed that *choosing* to be childfree affords women an

opportunity to define feminine identity separate from motherhood. Thus far, the research

has explored why some women have made the decision to be without children; however,

it has not yet investigated how this choice has affected their identity as women. Also

absent from the literature is an exploration of the factors that may support or threaten the

identity of women who have chosen not to be mothers. It would be important to understand more about the experience of women who choose not to have children, the response of others to their decision, and the impact of their decision on their sense of self.

Understanding more about the process of how women make the choice to not have children and how that decision affects their sense of themselves can provide important insights for clinicians working with these women. Many women who seek therapy or clinical support often do so around identity and life choice issues. An insecure sense of self and conflicts around identity may contribute to various psychological disorders, such as anxiety, depression, and substance use disorders. The potential stigmatization of women who have actively chosen not to have children and the impact of this decision on their self-esteem and identity, raise important clinical implications for therapists working with such clients.

This study explored the experience of women who have deliberately chosen not to have children. The study invited women between the ages of 25 to 40 who have made the decision to be without children to discuss how they have arrived at the decision and what their experience of the decision making process was like. The study investigated the ways in which this decision may relate to their sense of self and their overall identity as a woman.

In the following chapter, the review of the literature will examine the research pertaining to the prevalence of women without children, with particular attention paid to childfree women, that is, those women who have decided not to have children. The literature will examine their demographic profile, the process of their decision to not have children, the factors that played a role in influencing their choice, as well as their experience of living without children.

Chapter Three will describe the methodology of the research study. The research methodology involved semi-structured interviews of women, ages 25 to 40, who have decided not to have children. Chapter Four will provide the findings using a thematic analysis to uncover themes in the participants' experiences, highlighting the factors that led to their choice, as well as advantages and challenges of being without children. Lastly, Chapter Five will provide a discussion and interpretation of the findings highlighting the major, minor, and unexpected themes, strengths and limitations of the study, clinical implications, and identify areas for future research.

CHAPTER TWO

LITERATURE REVIEW

Despite the growing number of women who are voluntarily without children, cultural values around the world continue to uphold and revere parenting while women who choose not to have children are often dismissed and stigmatized. Social expectations and norms equate healthy adult female identity and development with motherhood. In this way, the terms *mother* and *woman* are frequently used interchangeably and those who do not conform experience social rejection (McQuillan, Greil, Shreffler, Wonch-Hill, Gentzler, & Hathcoat, 2012; Mollen, 2006). For example, according to Gillespie (2003), a website, TheNotMom website, celebrates women and men without children, and differentiates between the terms *childfree* and *childless*, suggesting that *childfree* be used for those who voluntarily made the choice to be without children, whereas *childless* be used for those who are involuntarily without children. For the purpose of this study, the research data examined will focus on women without children in the United States. The international data set is beyond the scope of this project.

Though the term childfree is used throughout this research project, it is acknowledged that the use of this term may imply that not having children is a virtue or advantage; however, as the literature suggests, childfree will be used to refer to those who have decided not to have children in the context of a fulfilling and active choice (Gillespie, 2003; McQuillan et al., 2012). Another term, transformative-childfree, has been used to refer to a strong commitment to childfreedom in the context of those who actively seek friends and partners who are in line with one's choice (McQuillan et al., 2012). In contrast, the term childless will refer to those who are involuntarily without

6

children for various reasons, that may include reproductive, physical, mental health, or financial challenges. Given the lack of clarity in differentiating what constitutes childlessness and childfreedom in some studies, when the research reviewed for this chapter fails to distinguish between the two, the phrase 'women who do not have children or women without children' will be used.

Although women's reasons for not having children are complex, society's perceptions of women without children are informed and maintained by gender role expectations. While the view of women as childbearers continues to pervade, it has been declining at a slow pace in recent years due to structural changes in the family composition, technological advances in reproduction, economic changes, as well as changes in cultural values (Hird & Abshoff, 2000; McQuillan et al., 2012). Historical and political changes in the United States and other countries in the past 40 years, including more effective birth control methods, accessible legal abortion, higher female education and employment rates, have contributed to the increase in women choosing to live without children (Gillespie, 2000). These changes have made it more acceptable for women to opt out of parenting (Gillespie, 2003; Hird & Abshoff, 2000; Shea, 1983).

Historical View of Children

Compared to modern Western relationships, marriage was not seen as the union between two people who wanted to be with each other due to love but rather as a way to increase one's socio-economic status through the acquisition and extension of land and properties (Gold, 2012; Hird & Abshoff, 2000). Procreation in preindustrial, agrarian society, was perceived as a method to increase the size of the family and thereby its financial fortunes, as there would be more individuals to work the land. In addition, children were recognized as a future economic resource, to be relied upon during old age. As such, children were valued for their economic contributions (Gillespie, 2003). They were seen as contributors and were often put to work by the age of five years. Mothers were not expected to focus their energies on raising children, as they are expected to in current society. For poorer and agrarian families, the more children they had, the more likely they were to increase their economic survival. Thus procreation was not only viewed in relation to maternal imperatives or instincts, but also in relation to the economic needs of the family (Gillespie, 2003; Gottlieb, 1993; Hird & Abshoff, 2000).

Several factors contributed to the changing view of motherhood in modern Western society. As families became less agrarian and less dependent on all members contributing to the economic survival of the family, adults were increasingly influenced by religious imperatives during the 15th and 16th centuries. Philosophical and social attitudes toward children changed (Wilson, 1984). Western societies began to emphasize those aspects of motherhood that had historically been influenced by religious ideals and had regarded motherhood as a divine blessing and affirmation of commitment to God (Gillespie, 2000; Gottlieb, 1993). By the 18th century, children were no longer viewed as economic contributors but as *tabula rasa* or "blank slates" and innocent beings, in need of moral and spiritual parental guidance, which only they could provide (Gottlieb, 1993; Wilson, 1984).

Furthermore, with the economic and political changes brought on by industrialization, coupled with the changes in religious and social organizations, Western societies began to separate out familial responsibilities pertaining to the productive and the reproductive spheres of life. The new philosophies of gender, in responding to middle class gender roles as well as more general economic changes, emphasized a view in which men (and fathers) were situated within the productive realm outside of the family, whereas women were seen as nurturers, situated in the home with a focus on rearing children and domestic tasks within the home (Schnucker, 1980 as cited in Hird & Abshoff, 2000).

Consequently, the role of parents changed and they became responsible to provide their children financial stability and emotional well-being (Hird & Abshoff, 2000). Children and adolescents were no longer perceived as providing economic stability but instead were expected to provide joy and emotional fulfillment to parents. Marriages also came to be viewed as a partnership based on choice and companionship. Emotional rather than economic factors became the dominant rationale for having children since they were no longer financial contributors, but instead were a source of financial burden. According to Zelizer, (cited in Hird & Abshoff, 2000), "children are economically worthless but emotionally priceless" (p.350).

Prevalence of Women Without Children

A 2015 Google search for the term "childfree" yielded 726,000 results, suggesting the topic has received wide attention from newspaper and other media sources. These findings suggest that, while the experience of women who choose to be without children were often overlooked or dismissed in the past, in recent years, this has become a topic of interest in the United Kingdom and the United States (Giles et al., 2009; Wayne, 2015).

Approximately one in five American women currently go through their childbearing years without having children, whereas, in the 1970s, one in ten women were without children (Livingston & Cohn, 2010). This statistic has been consistent over the past 20 years and across industrialized countries (Lee & Gramotnev, 2006). While

the prevalence of remaining without children for women occurs among all racial and

ethnic groups, it is more prevalent among women with higher education and advanced

degrees. A statistical analysis on the prevalence of women without children in the United

States by Livingston and Cohn (2010), based on data from the June fertility supplement

of the Census Bureau's Current Population Survey, demonstrated that the women most

likely not to bear children are those who have never married and those with advanced

degrees. According to a more recent study by Livingston (2015), there was an exception

to this rising trend in the years 1994 to 2008, whereby 31% of women aged 40 to 44

years with a master's, doctoral or professional degree did not have children compared to

24% in 2008. It is understood that this decline in the prevalence of those with advanced

degrees occurred as a result of some of these women having children, but delaying the

age at when they do so.

Livingston and Cohn (2010) posited that some women who desire to have

children end up without children due to unsuccessful pregnancy related to older age. The

authors also acknowledged that, according to an analysis of data from the National

Survey of Family Growth, the number of women aged 40 to 44 years who are voluntarily

without children is equal to those who are involuntarily without children. In 2002,

among women in that age group, 6% were deemed voluntarily childless, 6% involuntarily

childless, and 2% childless but hoping to have children in the future (Livingston & Cohn,

2010).

Despite a decline in marriage rates in the past decade, women who have never

married are still the most likely to be without children; however, the rate of women without children who are married or were at one point has risen (Livingston & Cohn, 2010).

Reasons provided for the increase in women who do not have children include declines in social pressure to have children, and related increased beliefs that bearing children is an individual choice (Livingston, 2015). These beliefs are primarily the result of the Women's Liberation movement which played a significant role in decreasing the disparity between the role of women and men both in the workforce and at home (Shea, 1983). Additionally, improved access to contraceptive methods and abortion, as well as greater job opportunities for women have helped create alternatives for those who remain without children. Most significant, is the age of women studied. Such research needs to take into account the increasing delay in childbearing among the highly educated in contrast to women who continue to remain without children.

Demographic Profile of Women who are Voluntarily Without Children

Given the prevalence of women who do not have children, one might wonder whether there is similarity among them in terms of demographic profile. While the literature suggests that White, middle- and upper-class women make up the majority of women without children in industrialized countries, Livingston & Cohn (2010) noted a different pattern. They found that not only were there a large proportion of women without children in various ethnic and racial groups, but also across a range of socioeconomic statuses.

Race and Ethnicity

Though the number of women without children is increasing, the proportion of Latino and Black women without children is slightly smaller than the proportion of White women. The statistics are more prevalent among Whites, at 20% and those with higher education, compared to 17% of African-American women and Latinas and 16% of Asians (Livingston & Cohn, 2010). However, this represented less than earlier numbers suggested because between 1994 and 2008, the rates were significantly higher for nonwhites than for Whites. During those years, the rate of Blacks and Latinas who had no children increased by more than 30%, whereas that of Whites rose by only 11%, thereby decreasing the racial discrepancy. Despite the racial disparity, the proportion of women without children has escalated because there has been an increase in the number of younger women without children overall (Livingston & Cohn, 2010; Livingston, 2015).

According to Livingston and Cohn (2010), based on data from the United States Census Bureau's population survey, the rate of not having children for White women ages 40-44 increases at each level of achieved education. Similarly, among Latinas, the share of women without children increases at each level of education achieved. However, for Black women, there is considerably less variation between those with different education levels. In contrast to the Livingston and Cohn (2015) data, a study by Lundquist, Budig, and Curtis (2009) reported very little to no difference between Black and White women in terms of educational attainment. These authors found that both Black and White women who are without children tend to be highly educated.

Socioeconomic Status

A study by McQuillan et al. (2012) in which 1,180 women without children were interviewed about their reasons for not having children, found that these women had higher family income when compared to women who had children. The second wave of feminism that occurred toward the end of 1960s to 1970s probably rendered it easier for women to decide to remain without children. In addition, increased access to birth control and to abortion may have enabled women who in the past would have had no choice but to bear children when pregnant, to actively choose not to do so. These factors likely further contributed to the drop in fertility rate.

Age and Education

Consistent with the above findings, Gold (2012), Park (2005), and Gillespie (2003) found that women who are without children tend to be more educated, have managerial or professional positions, and have relatively high incomes. Morell (2000) interviewed 34 married women who voluntarily chose to remain without children and found that three-quarters of them came from poor or working-class families. These women often linked their upward mobility to their decision to be without children.

A study by Martin and Kendig (2012) used census data collected from 2004 through 2009 for 885 women ages 25 to 40 years. The authors found that 35% of United States women, regardless of race or ethnicity with a four-year college degree or above were without children, compared to 15.6% of women with no college degree.

Park (2005) and Doyle, Pooley, and Breen (2015) also corroborated that women without children are more likely to be women who are highly educated, although Livingston (2015) noted that some women with advanced degrees have children later in life, after they have started their career and their income has increased. In relation to this, Livingston (2015) found a decline in the rate of American women without children who have advanced degrees at the end of their childbearing years. In 2005, the rate of women ages 40 to 44 who had never given birth was 20%, nine years later, in 2014, this rate dropped to 15%. This drop in the prevalence of older women without children may be due to increased support for parents in the workplace, changing attitudes regarding adoption, and expanded interventions to increase and extend fertility for women. This may have expanded the possibilities for women to become mothers in their late 30s and 40s. Livingston (2015) offered that while the rate of women without children has declined for women with advanced degrees at the end of their childbearing years, it has increased for younger women since the 1970s. She attributed the increase in the prevalence of women without children to delayed childbearing in the pursuit of educational goals, participation in the paid labor workforce, and the recent economic recession.

Looking specifically at the data for U.S. women over 40 years old, The Pew Research Center's (2010) census data, based on the June fertility supplement of the Census Bureau's Current Population Survey from 1992 to 1994 and 2006 to 2008 referred to as "1994" and "2008" respectively, revealed that in 2008, 24% of women ages 40-44 with a bachelor's degree or above did *not* have children, compared to 18% with some or no college degree and 17% for high school graduates and 15% for those without a high school diploma. Moreover, the longitudinal data revealed that, since the 1990s, the rate of women without children has increased more for the least educated women (Livingston & Cohn, 2010).

Relationship Status

There is an increasing subset of women without children who are lesbian or bisexual. It must be recognized that many lesbian women may have had children in the context of marriages and relationships with male partners, prior to 'coming out'.

Notwithstanding this, historically lesbians have been expected to be without children. This has decreased as opportunities and attitudes regarding bearing children in the context of a lesbian relationship have changed. The literature has not addressed the prevalence of voluntarily childless lesbians, those who have intentionally decided not to have children. Rather, the literature has focused on lesbians who want to become parents; as such, future research could address voluntary childfreedom in the lesbian community (Morell, 2000).

Pew Research Center's (2010) census data also suggested that married couples in the United States who choose not to have children are on the rise. Based on the Census Bureau's Current Population Survey data in Livingston and Cohn's (2010) study, in 2008, 13% of women aged 40 to 44 years who were currently married or were at one point had no children of their own compared to 11% in 1994, a small increase. In contrast, among women aged 40 to 44 who never married, 56% were without children in 2008 compared to 71% in 1994, a significant increase. In Martin and Kendig's (2012) study, the authors found that among women who do not have children with lower educational attainment, 19.2% of them were single and 35.3% were married or in cohabiting unions.

Rates of married women without children have increased especially for those with less than a college education. Livingston and Cohn (2010), based on data from the National Survey of Family Growth, reported that from 1994 to 2008, the prevalence of married women without children grew sharply for women ages 40-44 with less than a high school diploma or some college education. However, for married women who have a college education, the rate remained unchanged.

Family of Origin

Although previous studies had failed to find a significant link between family history and the decision to remain without children (Bram, 1974; Lipman-Blumen, 1972 as cited in Houseknecht, 1979; Ory, 1976), Houseknecht (1979) identified more subtle factors that may play a role in women's decision to not have children. Houseknecht (1979) compared subsets of 51 currently married women who were voluntarily without children and did not intend to have any in the future. Women who had made the decision relatively early in life, prior to meeting their husband or marrying, were referred to as *early articulators*. Women who arrived at the decision to remain without children later in life, after marriage and after having developed a preference for a lifestyle without children, were referred to as *postponers*. The early articulators were more likely to report greater psychological distance between themselves and their parents during adolescence. While both early articulators and postponers described moderate overall family warmth in their family of origin, the early articulators' ratings of family warmth were significantly lower than those of the postponers. Based on the research findings, the author suggested the possibility that the early articulators did not want to perpetuate family experiences characterized by the limited family warmth and attitude incompatibility experienced in their own family of origin.

Moreover, the early articulators reported that their parents, particularly their mothers, had stressed achievement efforts more than those of the postponers. Houseknecht (1979) posited that it may be that parents of the early articulators encouraged achievement more strongly which rendered the women less concerned with the idea of motherhood and more concerned about demonstrating success in activities deemed more valuable by their families, for which they would be recognized. In contrast, the postponers characterized their parents as encouraging of assertive autonomy. It is possible that the postponers were not as initially decisive about remaining without children given that they received more warmth from their family of origin and did not experience the psychological distance experienced by the early articulators. However, Houseknecht (1979) offered that when the postponers had a reason not to have children, (.e.g., achievement activities outside the home), they may have decided based on what they considered to be in their best interest given that they had grown up with parents who valued assertive autonomy. This socio-psychological study also revealed that the postponers had higher rates of social approval for choosing not to have children. It is important to note that Houseknecht's findings are based on an earlier publication and research study done in 1979; as such, it remains unclear to what extent this data is applicable in the current generation. While several studies have touched on women's decision-making process in relation to their early socialization and family of origin (Gold 2012; Hird & Abshoff, 2000; Mollen, 2006; Park, 2005; Pearce, 2002), they have not focused on the interaction between the two. In addition, although Houseknecht's study looked at family of origin and decision-making process, it did not explain how family of origin plays a role in why some women may choose not to have children. Instead, the study's focus was on the timing of the decision with more data provided about women who make this choice early on in life.

While there is not one pattern for choosing to remain without children, growing up in an environment that is relatively lacking in warmth and achievement-oriented, may provide a context which encourages women to consider alternative roles outside the home and may foster an earlier awareness of the advantages of a childfree lifestyle.

Perceptions of Womanhood and Relationship to Motherhood

Motherhood is often a key component in social definitions of the role of women and their identity. A dominating traditional perception of feminine identity views it in relation to a woman's reproductive function. For those who link womanhood and motherhood, women who choose to be without children are perceived as rejecting their femininity and natural adult role as a woman (Brandalesi & Bernardi, 2013; Doyle et al., 2015; Gold, 2012; Hird & Abshoff, 2000). The link between women and childbearing is such that it is often unquestioningly assumed that all women are natural mothers. As such, the relationship between women and reproduction may create additional challenges for women who choose to reject motherhood.

Views of Women Without Children

Despite the increasing number of women who are voluntarily without children, Livingston and Cohn (2010) noted that 38% of Americans reported this change as having a negative impact on society compared to 29% in 2007. These statistics are based on a 2009 Pew Research Center poll survey of 1,003 adults that included parents, people who intend to have children and those who do not intend to become parents. Although the authors did not explain in what ways the people polled perceived the impact to be negative, other studies either reported or alluded to the idea that it disrupts social order because women are thought to be nurturers (Gillespie, 2000; Hird and Abshoff (2000).

Women who choose to be childfree are often portrayed as valuing their career more than having children. In Mueller and Yoder's (1999) study on the perceptions and

18

stigmatization of non-normative family size status, 60 married women, ages 50 years or younger but predominantly White and generally well educated with an average of 16.15 years of education were interviewed on their experiences. Fifteen of these women were voluntarily childless and intended to remain so and the others were referred to as either super-normative mothers (having 4 or more children), normative mothers, and mothers with one child. The voluntary women without children in the study reported being perceived by other women as wanting to be like men who choose to devote their lives to their work. In a study by Vinson et al. (2010) in which 224 female students ages 18 to 40 years from an undergraduate psychology course at a predominantly public women's university in a southwestern state were interviewed about their perceptions of women who are voluntarily without children, including the role of ethnicity. These authors, Gillespie (2000) and Reading and Amatea (1986) as cited in Hird and Abshoff in 2000 offered that women who do not consider parenthood as their central life-goal were seen as having some type of psychological disturbance caused by either childhood trauma, being parentified at a young age, having poor parental role models, or not having an emotionally close relationship to their mothers. The authors noted that these conclusions were based on earlier studies conducted prior to the Women's Liberation movement. However, these conclusions were not generalizable as the sample sizes were not only small but also subject to selection bias given it was not randomized. The participants were predominantly White and upper class (May, 1995).

Park (2002) studied the experience of 24 voluntarily childfree women and men to explore the way in which they manage stigma about their choice and preserve a good sense of identity. She found that the women reported being perceived as selfish, cold, materialistic, more driven, less caring, less emotionally healthy, lower in warmth, peculiar, and abnormal. These findings were also reflected in McQuillan et al.'s (2012) study who looked at 1,180 women without children ages 25 to 45 years, based on the 2005 Current Population Survey, about their reasons not to have children as well as Mueller & Yoder's (1999) study of 60 married voluntary childfree women ages 50 years or younger and their perceptions of how others perceive them. Some of the participants in Mueller and Yoder's study reported experiencing covert, yet hurtful statements or direct insults by other women about not having children. In addition to being criticized, the women also reported being pitied.

Mollen (2006) conducted a study in which nine voluntarily childfree women ages 32 to 51 years in a Midwest state were interviewed about the reasons they chose not to have children and the responses received from others about their choice. Respondents reported that some people treated their choice to be without children as a form of social deviance while others assumed their decision to be temporary. They described being told by other women that they would change their mind later and would eventually feel the maternal urge. In Doyle, Pooley, and Breen's (2015) study in which ten Australian women who were voluntarily childfree were interviewed about their choice and its consequences, some reported being told that they were different or weird, and that they were not natural or normal.

According to various authors (Mollen, 2006; Mueller & Yoder, 1999), based on their research, women face social pressure to have children and are encouraged to procreate for different reasons. Some of these reasons include not regretting their decision, owing their parents grandchildren, or not being lonely in their old age as children would provide company and support. This pressure was reported to come from family, friends, co-workers/colleagues, acquaintances, gynecologists/physicians, and sometimes even strangers. For married couples, this pressure was reported to start in their third or fourth year of marriage, peaking at the seventh year.

While voluntarily childfree women have increasingly gained acceptance in society, they continue to experience varying degrees of stigma. A study by Giles, Shaw, and Morgan (2009) in which 116 articles published from 1990 to 2008 in British newspapers noted that the media in the United Kingdom portray women who do not have children as selfish and uncaring. The researchers determined this by analyzing the newspapers and identifying themes based on how the news articles were presented on voluntary childlessness. The data was then combined together to produce a set of 15 frames that best characterized their sample. Likewise, surveys of students, parents, and the general public, conducted in the United States and in the United Kingdom also continue to depict women without children as deviant, undesirable, empty, and unfeminine (Doyle et al., 2015; Gillespie, 2003; Malacrida et al., 2012). For example, Doyle's (2015) study which explored the experiences of 10 women in Australia ages 32 to 53 who do not have children noted that the women reported that their choice to be without children were perceived by family members and others in their social network as a socially deviant act. Additionally, the women reported being subjected to pressure to have children. Similarly, Malacrida and Boulton's (2012) study in which they interviewed 21 women in England without children ages 18 to 31 as well as 22 women who had given birth in the past 18 months ages 24 to 40 to explore their perceptions of choice and birthing found that both women without children and women who did not have a vaginal birth were perceived as selfish and lazy. It is important to note that some these studies included relatively small sample sizes; as such, they should be interpreted carefully as they may not represent the experiences of all women without children.

View of Couples who do not Have Children

Although couples who have intentionally decided not to have children are often perceived negatively by those who have or aspire to have children, some couples report that they have received more support in recent years than when they were in the process of deciding (Brandalesi & Bernardi, 2013). This may represent a societal shift in that childfree couples' choice not to have children is more acceptable than it was in the past. Alternatively, it may also suggest that couples receive more support after they have made the decision rather than while deciding.

Given social and political changes in attitudes about the decision not to have children over the past 40 years, it is now more possible for such couples to feel more legitimate and less vulnerable about their choices (Gillespie, 2003). This trend was also noted by Chancey and Dumay (2009) who found that couples who have chosen to not have children are portrayed more positively than they once were in marriage and family textbooks. These authors described how previous studies had depicted voluntarily childfree couples as selfish and portrayed parents as brave for undertaking the task of parenting.

Time Spent With Children

Even though some women are without children – be it adopted, foster or step children - they may be very involved with children in their personal lives. A study by Martin and Kendig (2012) examined time spent with children in a sample of 885 women in young to middle adulthood. The authors investigated separately the time diaries of women with their own children (e.g., adopted, foster, or step-children) and those without their own children (e.g., children of friends or relatives) to assess the proportion of their weekly time spent with children. They noted that of the 701 women without children of their own, the college graduates were less likely to spend time with children and more likely to work longer hours (45 hours or more) than the women with less education.

The authors suggested that the extra hours spent at work provided life satisfaction and a sense of generativity that these women might have otherwise gained from spending time with children. For women with lower educational attainment, however, working longer hours was less likely to provide this type of satisfaction and they were more likely to spend free time with children. Among the explanations for the disparities in time spent with children, Martin and Kendig (2012) offered the possibility that women without a four-year college degree, and who have no children, may be spending time with children of their own siblings, their partner's siblings or children of relatives. For the higher educational attainment group, the authors offer the possibility that these women's siblings, their partners' siblings or relatives, were more likely to also be college graduates, either postponed having children or intentionally choosing to be without children thereby, providing less opportunity to be around children. It is important to note though that a limitation of this study is that it did not discern whether these women were voluntarily without children or not.

Changing Attitudes Toward Those Who Decide not to Have Children

Over the past few decades, negative and judgmental attitudes regarding those couples who decide not to have children have changed and childfreedom has become somewhat more accepted (Mueller & Yoder, 1999; Park, 2005). According to the General Social Survey (cited in Livingston & Cohn, 2010), the percentage of people who thought couples who do not have children do not live empty lives was 39% in 1988 versus 59% in 2002, a significant increase. It is important to note that although this indicates a decrease in the negative view of childfreedom, 41% of people surveyed in a sample of 2765 women may have viewed couples without children as living 'empty' lives. In addition, the research indicates that increasingly children are considered less essential to a successful marriage. In a 2007 survey by the Pew Research Center, it was found that 65% of adults stated children to be very important to a good marriage in 1990, but this number has decreased to 41% in 2007. This decline was also reflected in other industrialized nations (Livingston & Cohn, 2010; Santo, 2010).

A more recent study by Rowlands and Lee (2006), conducted with 119 first-year psychology students and members of the general public, with the majority of the sample being women under age 20 in Australia on their perceptions of heterosexual and lesbian women who do not have children and mothers, suggested that although this view still persists, attitudes have changed slightly. In this study, the authors found that the participants in their sample, overall, perceived women who are mothers, particularly heterosexual mothers more positively than women without children and lesbian mothers. However, mothers were also rated as less happy, less mature, and less individualistic than women without children. This suggests that while mothers are perceived more positively, they are not necessarily seen as being happy, mature, or individualistic. Similarly, participants viewed lesbian mothers, as compared to lesbians who did not have children, as happier, more mature, and more individualistic. The researchers posited the possibility that because lesbians face more difficulties to become mothers and have likely had to

weigh many aspects in making that choice, they are viewed more positively than those

who are not mothers. This suggests that attitudes towards lesbian motherhood may be

changing. It is important to note that these results were based on a limited sample of 119

people of which the majority of participants were female, students, under 20 years, were

European, Australian, and single. Students tend to be more liberal in their views and, as

such, the study might have yielded different results if conducted with a more

heterogeneous or older population.

Women Without Children's Sense of Self

According to Mueller and Yoder (1999), previous research on the identity of

women without children has shown that these women develop positive identities only

after they have passed their childbearing years as opposed to during these years. In other

words, women without children were thought to develop a good sense of self after they

reached menopause because they were no longer able to bear children and therefore,

could no longer be ambivalent about their choice. Increasingly, the research indicates

that women who have chosen not to have children experience a sense of fulfillment

before their childbearing years end. Current research has suggested that women, whether

single or in a romantic relationship, women without children travel, spend time with

extended families, and engage in activities they deem enjoyable and fulfilling (Mueller &

Yoder, 1999; Peterson & Engwall, 2013).

Childfreedom in Popular Culture as Reflected in the Media

Childfreedom has gained popularity over the past two decades and it has become

common for newspapers and various media sources to publish articles on the topic. In a study by Giles et al. (2009) analyzing 116 newspaper articles published on childfreedom in the United Kingdom between 1990 and 2008, the results indicated that for the most part the decision to be without children was portrayed negatively (e.g., as selfish, uncaring). However, some articles were seen to depict the choice to be without children as a woman's rights issue (i.e. feminist liberation).

The authors also analyzed how the newspapers framed the issue and found four dominant themes. The first theme related to human right issues in which the discourse explicitly stated that women have the right to remain without children. A second theme compared parents to non-parents and portrayed childfreedom as social deviance and argued against the choice to be without children. A third theme involved the media portrayal of childfreedom as a symptom of social change, and tended to use statistics to compare current figures of women without children with those in previous decades, blaming the government and labor force for valuing long work hours making it difficult for women to balance both work and parenting. The fourth theme depicted childfreedom as a personal decision rather than a political or socioeconomic choice, and asked rhetorically whether or not it was the right decision made (Giles et al., 2009).

Some authors have argued that the language used in the media to refer to childfreedom tends to assume a deficit stance. They argue that terms such as non-mother, without children, childfree, and childless, imply a deficit identity (Doyle et al., 2015; Gold, 2012). Each of these terms implies the violation of norms or social expectations that privilege the value of children and motherhood. These authors argue that this vocabulary tends to either problematize (childless) or glorify not having children (childfree) (Gillespie, 2003; Gold, 2012; McQuillan et al., 2012).

Psychological Health and Motherhood

There are different perspectives on the view that being a parent is implicated in adult mental health. Erik Erikson's multiple stage theory (1963) of development characterized the stage of middle adulthood as dominated by themes of generativity versus stagnation. In this stage, procreation was privileged as a means of achieving generativity, although Erikson recognized that generativity could also be achieved via holding a leadership role in society. Without this, adults were seen as failing to reach their full potential and were viewed as psychologically stagnant, unless they contributed to positive changes that benefits others. In the context of Freud's oedipal theory, he viewed becoming a mother, and having a baby of her own, to be a critical means through which a woman could resolve some key elements of early development, particularly her discovery of female gender, and the absence of the penis. Although challenged by contemporary theorists, psychoanalytic perspectives on gender identity emphasized the relationship between sexual reproduction, feminine gender identity and psychic health. According to Lee and Gramotnev (2006), this association implied that a woman who did not achieve motherhood had failed to accept her own quintessence and had failed to adequately resolve her psychological conflicts from childhood.

Empirical evidence, however, has refuted this view as there is little to no evidence of psychological maladjustment or lack of generativity for women who opt out of motherhood. A study by Lee and Gramotnev (2006) compared the psychological functioning of 678 Australian women between the ages of 22 to 27 years. The authors found little social or psychological differences between those who desired children versus those who did not. Likewise, as cited in a Doyle et al.'s (2015) study, Rothauff and

Cooney (2008) compared 289 people without children to 2218 parents in the United States in terms of their generativity development and psychological well-being and found no difference. This finding was also demonstrated in Koropeckyj-Cox's (2002) study in which the well-being of 3135 parents and individuals without children were compared, ages 50 to 84 years. Koropeckyj-Cox and DeLyser (2011) suggested that when the decision was voluntary, women without children were not regretful of their decision, neither were they unhappy. Several women without children reported seeing motherhood as a burden and a social duty they were not interested in pursuing (Doyle et al., 2015; Hird & Abshoff, 2000).

In Doyle et al.'s (2015) study of 10 women who chose to be without children, the women reported being proud of their identities. They described how they were able to engage in generative activities in their careers, do volunteer work, and be involved in their extended families. The authors offered that these women's descriptions contradicted the stereotype of women who do not have children as being selfish and suggested that these women were fulfilling Erikson's generative stage of development by contributing to the betterment of others. Many of the women in the study were employed in the helping professions and all reported to have more time for themselves as well as being available to help others. However, one woman added that she felt badly about not having children and felt compelled to help others as a way to give something back to society for her lack of reproduction (Doyle et al., 2015).

Contemporary Perceptions of Women's Identity in Relation to Motherhood

The second wave of feminism, beginning in the 1960s and 1970s, was an impetus for changed attitudes about gender roles. The women's rights movement sought to re-examine social attitudes because they were based upon what had been assumed as scientifically validated knowledge on sex roles. The increased number of women in the paid workforce, as well as increased options for contraception introduced new possibilities for fulfillment other than motherhood. More women joined the labor force, married later in life, and delayed childbearing. As such, childbearing has come to lose its organizing social value and plays a less central role in some women's lives (Shea, 1983; Vinson et al., 2010; Wortis, 1971).

Hird and Abshoff (2000) have drawn attention to Simone de Beauvoir's assertion that patriarchal discourse, which attributed women's essence to anatomical sex differences, could be challenged to reveal gender to be a social construct, and not a biological category. Feminists have argued that, for women, gender identity is based on their ability to reproduce and to be mothers, whereas men's identity is attained through their occupational status, economic success, and sexual prowess (Hird & Abshoff, 2000; Peterson & Engwall, 2013).

It is important to note that the overarching goal of feminism is not to completely abandon motherhood. Rather, feminists have encouraged autonomy over women's right to reproduce as well as the right to safe access to birth control and abortion (Gillespie, 2000; Hird & Abshoff, 2000; Shea, 1983). They have challenged the notion that motherhood should obstruct the participation of women in education and in the workforce. Additionally, feminists have advocated for enhanced and alternative child-care services that would allow mothers more opportunity to fully participate in the workforce; and they have fought for maternity benefits and equal pay.

Furthermore, feminists have challenged the devaluation of mothers and the submissive role women are assigned in the family system. Given that most women continue to bear children, feminist theory has encouraged greater awareness of the impact maternity has on women's identities (Doyle et al., 2015; Hird & Abshoff, 2000). Feminists have argued that motherhood is seen as an institution which builds specific ideas about the female body and places certain expectations on women's behavior, while changing and constraining their identity as women. In this way, the ability to bring new life into the world is used to both revere women while also confining and limiting them for being mothers (Hird & Abshoff, 2000).

A Complex Picture of Choice

Some women described in the literature have had difficulty formulating a clear motive for their decision not to have children. In a study of 23 voluntarily childfree women and men, including couples, ages 31 to 56 years old, Park (2005) asked the respondents why they did not have or want to have children. Both the women and the men, regardless of marital status, struggled to provide a clear answer but they nevertheless described their choice as obvious and natural. In some instances, authors have described childfreedom as a non-conscious choice. To illustrate this, in their interviews with 30 women in Sweden, ages 29 to 64 years who do not have children on their experiences, one woman interviewed by Peterson and Engwall (2013) stated she could not ever recall making the decision not to have children; she stated "it's not correct to call it a decision. I've never imagined myself as a parent or as having kids" (p.381). Another woman stated "I have no biological signals or biological urge or a ticking clock. One would think that it's in our biological body … that our body would signal when you see a child" (p.381). Another woman reported, "it's something you don't choose. I think it's genetic" (p.381). From these responses it seems that some women, may assume that the desire to have children involves a biological imperative, that for them is absent or lacking.

Multiple studies on childfreedom have explored the reasons why women actively choose not to have children. People who are voluntarily without children are a heterogeneous group and their reasons for making this decision vary, sometimes significantly. From a feminist academic perspective, Hird and Abshoff (2000) have explored voluntary childfree women's experiences. They argue that the reasons women commonly cite for remaining without children are preserving freedom, pursuing education, pursuing career and economic opportunities, protecting the intimacy in their marital relationships, resisting gender role stereotypes; disliking children; early familial and childhood experiences; apprehensions regarding the process of childbearing; concerns about world overpopulation; anxiety about their ability to raise children emotionally and financially; and not having the "right" partner and the "right" environment (Hird & Abshoff, 2000) Additional authors (Giles et al., 2009; Mollen, 2006; Park, 2005) have supported these stated reasons.

Freedom. Freedom has been cited as the most common reason why individuals without children make that choice. This motivation has been reported in studies of couples without children done in the United States, Canada, Scotland, the United Kingdom, Australia, and New Zealand. Moreover, these studies have explored the experiences of younger and older women and men, single and coupled who do not have children (Doyle et al., 2015; Gillespie, 2003; Hird & Abshoff, 2000; Park, 2005).

Couples have described their ability to center their lives around adult activities including having personal independence over their time, the flexibility to move about and to attend to their opportunities more freely, to be spontaneous about their desires and pursuits, as well as the ability to be self-determined (Gold, 2012; Hird & Abshoff, 2000; Mollen, 2006). Some women, regardless of marital status, saw the freedom to travel and to experience the world without constraint or compromise as essential to their life style that would not be available with motherhood. For example, a woman in Doyle et al.'s (2015) study stated that she felt fortunate to have the freedom to explore herself and her life. For these women, motherhood was sometimes viewed as impeding freedom, time-consuming, and a burden. A woman in Gillespie's (20003) study reported that she arrived at her decision to be without children by observing others; she stated:

> I want to travel a lot more. I like a lot of time to myself. I like to read. I like to sew. I design my own clothes. You can't do that when you've got children. Yes, it's the time to myself. … It means having the freedom, within certain restrictions, to say I am going to do that now; I am going to do that tomorrow; that next year; and know that I can. All I have got to do is to go home and say to my husband. … I don't have to consider anyone else. Also not having this feeling of resentment of not being able to do something because someone else is making demands on my time (p.127).

Educational and career goals. Another common reason not to have children was educational and career opportunities and goals. Women without children often note conflicts that come with trying to combine employment with motherhood. They see motherhood as a compromise between family and career aspirations, which their male counterparts do not have to entertain. Furthermore, they view parenthood as costing a lot and yielding little satisfaction (Gold, 2012; Lee & Gramotnev, 2006). In Park's (2005) interviews, women without children reported that they felt they would be unable to pursue their educational and career goals if they were mothers. They saw motherhood as a barrier that would prevent them the flexibility to devote their time to their education or career because children require time and attention. For this reason, some women felt they had to choose between being a parent or having a career. For some women, having a career was more important, as it would allow them the opportunity to be financially comfortable (Hird & Abshoff, 2000; Park, 2005). Brandalesi and Bernardi (2013) explored 68 single and coupled heterosexual women and men without children, ages 34 to 65 years and asked them to describe the meaning of their choice to not have children. Some couples stated that they saw the option of having children or a full-time job as an either/or choice.

Preserving intimacy of the couple. Another reason women have provided for being without children is the belief that children can interrupt the intimacy of couples. Park (2005) found this need to preserve marital intimacy more common among the women than the men in the eight couples without children she interviewed. Although the women reported their husbands as being supportive of their choice, Park (2005) and others found that the women were reportedly usually the ones to bring up the topic of not having children and to lead the decision (Gillespie, 2003; Lee & Zvonkovic, 2014). Further, some women in Park's (2005) study reported that they had made their decision after observing how children interfered with the leisure time of couples they knew. Several couples without children asserted that they had a closer relationship with their significant others than they thought their counterparts with children did because children constantly require time and attention, which reduces the couple's intimate time together. While research suggests that couples who do not have children do not necessarily view children as an absolute disruption to romantic relationships, they tended to see children as unnecessary to a union that was already experienced as gratifying (Hird & Abshoff, 2000;

Mollen, 2006). To illustrate this, a woman in Gillespie's (2003) study stated:

> It [having no children] conjures up being able to do exactly what I want and what
> my husband and I want to do as a couple. … It means I'm able to have a career
> and career ambitions rather than just a job, and it also means being able to give a
> lot more time to other relationships like my marriage, friendships. These are the
> things that make me happy, and I don't want to give them up (p.129).

DeLyser (2011), in a study of 15 intentionally childfree married or partnered

women, suggested that while some childfree couples view parenthood positively, they

often express satisfaction and contentment with their family of two. A woman in this

study stated she and her husband married not necessarily to have children but because of

their desire to be together. Others reported not feeling the need to have children in order

to make their relationship work, while others reported not feeling unfulfilled. Some

expressed concern about the adverse impact of children on the couples' relationship. To

illustrate, one woman reported that at the time she married her husband, "he really

wanted to have children. I said I thought it [having children] would destroy our

relationship. You work nights and I would be like a single mom. We would never have a

relationship" (p.71). This is consistent with other studies that have shown that the wish

to protect the intimacy of the couple is often a key motive in the decision to be without

children. DeLyser (2011), Gillespie (2003), and Park (2005) suggested that for some

women without children, their relationship with their husbands may mean more to them

than having children.

Rejecting traditional gender roles. According to Mollen (2006) in interviews of

nine voluntary childfree women ages 32 to 51 about why they had chosen to be without

children, several women described how they had always rejected prescribed gender roles and activities. Some reported they had not wanted to play with dolls or had played with them differently than their female friends or sisters had. Others identified themselves as tomboys growing up and reported being more interested in other activities, such as reading, playing outdoors, and playing games that were more exploratory or physical rather than the nurturing themes typical of female play (Mollen, 2006).

Hird and Abshoff (2000) found that people assume a primary reason women choose to be without children is because they dislike children. However, several authors have argued that this is a stereotype and there is little empirical evidence to support it (Hird, 2003; Martin & Kendig, 2012). In fact, childfree women's attitudes toward children vary. While some do vehemently dislike children and avoid their company, many devote time to children as aunts, godparents, or as teachers and child-care professionals (DeLyser, 2011; Martin & Kendig, 2012; Morell, 2000; Park, 2005). In a book by May (1995) in which she examined the intersection of public life, sexuality, procreation, and family, 61% of women without children were found to have frequent contact with children on a social basis, while 15% had contact with children within a work environment. These figures suggest that positive feelings and attitudes toward children are not predictors of motherhood; nor are they inextricably linked.

Early family experiences. For a minority of women without children, the decision not to have children can be explained in part by early socialization and childhood familial experiences (Park, 2005). Interestingly, however, there is no identifiable or unique experience in their childhood that differentiates them from parents. Gold (2012), in an article based on literature-based data exploring the experiences of childfree and childless couples, suggested that instead, it is their interpretations of these experiences that led to their decision to be without children. These experiences ranged from witnessing marital breakdown or their mother's unhappiness in her marital relationship, to having a handicapped or ill sibling or parent, or having elderly parents. Perceptions of their own families varied from seeing themselves as having parents who had been self-sacrificing, nurturing and extremely devoted, to having parents who had been primarily devoted to their careers. Some women explained how seeing their parents struggle to be an ideal family deterred them from wanting to have their own family because they saw this striving as a never-ending goal. Some women reported that having been responsible for younger siblings as they were growing up played a factor in deciding not to have children. They reported being parentified at an early age, which they said had prevented them from spending time with peers or engaging in activities they deemed enjoyable (Hird & Abshoff, 2000; Mollen, 2006). Some women also described witnessing traumatic experiences in their home or being victims of violence. These women expressed an equivocal desire to stop the generational cycles of abuse, supporting Doyle et al.'s (2015) finding that it is women who tend to stop this cycle. In these cases, the women said they did not want to put children through what they had experienced (Doyle et al., 2015).

Concerns about childbirth. Another reason sometimes provided for being without children had to do with the rigors of pregnancy and childbirth. Some women reported that the stress and fear of pregnancy and childbirth were reasons enough for them not to go through it (May, 1995). Some women in May's (1995) book reported being repulsed by the physical act of giving birth and referred to it as "messy" and "barbaric." They were reluctant to deal with the pain and discomfort of pregnancy and the lack of dignity during delivery or the demeaning medical treatment of pregnant women they associated with the process. More specifically, they said they felt as though they would have no control over their pregnancy and labor. Interestingly, women were not the only ones who expressed skepticism about the physical process of birth. Some husbands in Gold's (2012) study of the experiences of childfree and childless couples in the United States reported not wanting to see their wife or significant other experience the pain of childbirth. The author reported that this negative view of the physical demands of pregnancy and childbirth was usually related to previous exposure to or knowledge about difficult and traumatic pregnancies. Finally, women occasionally reported a fear of passing on genetically inheritable diseases or mental illness that ran in their families (Hird & Abshoff, 2000; Mollen, 2006).

Philanthropic concerns. Some women without children have identified philanthropic concerns as a factor in making their decision (Park, 2005). These concerns pertain to issues such as world overpopulation and such social problems as discrimination, bullying, child abuse, among others. For some, moral responsibility and pessimism about the future of the world were reason enough to keep them from having children. Some women reported fears that overpopulation would decrease the world's resources, especially given that people in industrialized countries already consume a large proportion of resources. Some asserted that their childfreedom prevented them from further contributing to a world that is already burdened and compromised (May, 1995 as cited in Hird & Abshoff, 2000; Park, 2005; Peterson & Engwall, 2013). Others have explained that they believed it was unfair and selfish to bring another being into an unwelcoming world, particularly if parents cannot afford to properly care for their children or secure them an adequate financial and emotional future.

Anxiety about parenting. Anxiety about parenting ability has also been cited by some authors (Gold, 2012; May, 1995; Park, 2005) as another reason some women and men choose to not have children. Some women interviewed by Park (2005) expressed fear that they would not be as good as their parents were, especially if they saw their parents' skills as exceptional. Conversely, others reported being afraid of repeating their parents' negative parenting skills or patterns (Gold, 2012; Park, 2005). Though these negative patterns did not necessarily include explicit abuse or neglect, they often involved witnessing their parents struggle financially to support the family, witnessing one of their parents, usually the mother, being unhappy, or seeing their parents struggle to balance their career and family life, often with their family life losing time over career demands (Hird & Abshoff, 2000; May, 1995). In Doyle et al.'s (2015) study of 10 voluntary childfree women, four women identified themselves as lacking emotional maturity or skills to have and raise children. They recognized the immense responsibility of raising children and did not believe they could manage the responsibility.

Some women state that having the "right" partner and the "right" environment (cohabitating) is important for them to procreate (Brandalesi & Bernardi, 2013). Regardless of marital status, some women in Brandalesi and Bernardi's (2013) study of 68 women and couples without children reported that they could have been mothers but the "opportunities" (being married) were not linked with other perceived "right" conditions (good relationship or partner) to become a parent at the time (Brandalesi & Bernardi, 2013).

Mezey (2013) and Rowlands and Lee (2006) explored how lesbians and gay men decide to have children or be childfree. Both studies found that some lesbian women's decision to be without children results from internalized homophobia due to heterosexist and homophobic messages they receive from society that suggest they would not be good parents and that their children would be damaged. As a result, they questioned their own right and ability to parent. In addition, because some lesbians did not feel legally protected, they hesitated to have children as they were afraid their children would not have legal protection (Baiocco & Fiorenzo, 2013; Mezey, 2013). Rowlands and Lee (2006) explained that due to some societies' strong legislative barriers for lesbians who desire to have children, many couples are not able to adopt a child jointly. As such, if the adoptive mother were to die, her partner would not have any legal responsibility for the child and her wish or decisions concerning that child may not be granted (Mezey, 2013).

As the motives mentioned above demonstrate, the decision to forego parenting is not simple but complex and diverse, and is often based on several interconnected factors. It will be important to re-explore these findings in light of the recent Supreme Court decision that has recently legalized lesbian and gay marriages throughout the country. Overall, the literature suggests that decision to live without children often develops over time and, contrary to the stereotypes, it is not typically made early in a woman's childbearing years. The following section will examine the decision-making process, the time frame, and how women and couples decide that they do not want to have children.

How Do Women Arrive at the Decision to be Without Children?

In a sample of 51 married women between the ages of 25 and 40 years, Houseknecht (1979) compared subsets of women who were voluntarily childfree.

Consistent with the extant literature, this study revealed that while the women could not identify the exact point in time when they had made the decision, they had no difficulty recalling whether or not they had decided prior to marriage or meeting their husband (Houseknecht, 1979). Moreover, these authors, as well as McQuillan et al. (2012), found postponement to be the more frequent path to being childfree. In contrast, later research by Doyle, Pooley and Breen (2015) and Gillespie (2003) found that early articulators made up the majority of the women in their studies. This suggests a possible shift in that women born after the second wave of feminism may be choosing to remain childfree earlier in life than had occurred in the past.

While some women report always knowing they did not want to have children, others describe defining events in their childhood or adolescence that have steered them in that direction (DeLyser, 2011).

Couples' Decision-Making About Not Having Children

One might wonder about the decision process of couples who choose not to have children. Lee and Zvonkovic (2014) interviewed 20 voluntarily childfree married couples and asked them how they had reached the decision. Their results revealed that for some couples, the decision was simple and short; however, for others, it was a longer process. Similar to Houseknecht's (1979) earlier study about different types of voluntary women who choose not to have children, the authors identified three types of decision-making among couples: mutual early articulators, mutual postponers, and nonmutual couples. Additionally, they found two underlying forces that drive the process: the strength of conviction not to have children, and the importance of the couple relationship.

The mutual early articulator couples in Lee and Zvonkovic's (2014) study were those in which *both* partners knew they did not want to have children prior to being married. Such couples reportedly tended to arrive at the decision painlessly and fairly quickly as both partners knew they did not want to be parents early on and had discussed it prior to getting married. However, occasionally, the couples revisited the topic to be sure both parties were happy with their decision. The mutual postponer couples were reportedly ambivalent about having children and reported that they had never gotten to having children for various reasons. Similar to the mutual early articulators, these couples arrived at the decision easily and revisited the topic from time to time to ensure both parties were satisfied with the status quo, demonstrating the importance of the relationship.

The nonmutual couples were those in which one partner wanted to have a child or was ambivalent but the other partner did not want a child. These couples took longer to arrive at their decision because they wanted to be sure that they took their partners' feelings into consideration and often revisited the topic. The partners with the strong conviction not to have children usually conveyed the message that having children would be a "deal breaker" and if the relationship was important enough, then they would agree to not have children.

Interestingly, as Gillespie (2003) has also observed, these authors found that women were more likely to bring up the discussion about being without children, though some men did as well (Lee & Zvonkovic, 2014). These studies, as well as the one by Brandalesi and Bernardi (2013), demonstrate that the decision for couples to remain without children is a process and that couples who do so may take account of the importance of the relationship and engage in a decision-making process over a period of time. The research, particularly the study by Houseknecht (1979), indicates that although some couples may choose to voluntarily not have children, for some this may not be an easy decision, and may be characterized by some ambivalence and conflict.

Diversity and Cultural Factors in Decision Making

Sexual orientation does not preclude some women from facing the decision about bearing children. Increasingly lesbian women and gay men are forming families and deciding whether to have children or remain without. Like heterosexual women who choose not to have children, some lesbians who value economic and personal freedom choose to be without children, especially when their jobs afford them such freedom. They report being afraid that becoming a mother would impede their freedom. However, Riskind and Patterson (2010) and Baiocco and Fiorenzo (2013) both explored the parenting intentions, attitudes, and desires of lesbian, gay, and heterosexual individuals without children. They found that lesbians were less likely to express the desire or intention to become parents than heterosexual women even though both groups valued motherhood (Mezey, 2013; Riskind & Patterson, 2010). These findings suggest that, like heterosexual women, for some lesbian women, the decision to not have children is not always the result of personal preference but may be the product of a complex interaction of legal, political and personal factors. Rather, lesbians carefully weigh their options given their perceived lack of support from family, partners, friends, and community members, as well as the stigmatization and overt legal, medical, and adoptive roadblocks they encounter in the larger community.

The accounts of lesbian women who choose not to have children as a result of these concerns and fears highlight the complexity of the issue faced for many women (and couples) who experience this as a difficult choice, not what they would ideally choose or wish but feel compelled to do by circumstances. Under these circumstances the decision to not have children does not reflect a self-affirming expression of identity and personal choice.

Race and Ethnicity

Research has shown that race and ethnicity contribute to perceptions of women who do not have children. A study by Vinson, Mollen, and Smith (2010) explored the impact of ethnicity on perceptions of women who are voluntarily childfree. The authors surveyed 224 female students in a psychology course at a public women's university and asked them to rate case vignettes of White women and women of color who were either mothers or were without children. The study demonstrated that White participants without children were rated negatively by all participants, but women of color without children were rated even more negatively. The authors suggested that this may be due to less flexible gender expectations for women of color. Vinson et al. (2010) speculated that because women of color are not expected to be without children, they may be judged more harshly. In contrast, all participants rated women of color who were mothers more positively than women of color without children. These authors speculated that child rearing may represent racial affirmation for African Americans due to historical contexts in which families were fragmented and some were subjected to forced sterilization (Lisle, 1996, as cited in Vinson et al., 2010). McQuillan et al. (2012) found that even though most voluntarily childfree women receive social pressure about having children, Black women received more.

Influence of Religion

The majority of religious traditions are pronatalistic; that is, they support and even encourage childbearing. From a young age, children of religious parents are exposed to messages that encourage reproduction and children may model their parents' attitudes (Pearce, 2002). Research has shown a strong association between religiosity and low acceptance of childfreedom (McQuillan et al., 2012). Some religions, such as Catholicism, forbid the use of contraception, thereby significantly constraining the long-term feasibility of maintaining a choice to not have children for most sexually active couples. Pearce (2002) noted that some religions such as Catholicism and Protestantism, especially conservative Protestantism, value parenthood for women more than they do education and career achievements. They consider parenthood to be a high calling and view children as God's gifts. They encourage reproduction by sponsoring family gatherings, offering parent classes, family counseling, and providing financial support for childcare services through their religious social networks. This in turn, keeps the family engaged in a culture that values reproduction. In this way, the more that parents attend religious services, the more exposure they receive from their church and internalize messages about family composition, the more they pass them on to their children (Pearce, 2002). However, while interviews find that women who have chosen not to have children tend to be less religious than mothers (Gillespie, 2003; Gold, 2012), Craig et al. (2014) found that the importance of religion is declining as a factor in women's choices.

Internalization of Cultural Gender Norms

Kroll (2011) has noted that while men are encouraged to participate in recreational activities and sports, women are more likely to be encouraged to join organizations related to health, social services, caring for others, or nurturing children. In this way, women and men, parents and non-parents have traditionally been assigned to different roles influenced by their gender identities. Feminist theorists, such as (Hird & Abshoff, 2000; Morell, 2000; Shea, 1983), who have offered a social critique of gender identity and roles in Western culture, have noted that a dominant view of motherhood regards it as a rite of passage to womanhood and brings with it enhanced social status and respect. Women are expected to be self-sacrificing and commit themselves to the role of parenting. In this view, pregnant women are seen as selfless, abandoning their childlike and self-absorbed selves to become a better version of themselves, a true adult woman. Sacrifice and pain of childbirth are associated with ideal womanhood and women who are not mothers are viewed as failing womanhood (Malacrida & Boulton, 2012). These feminist theorists have argued that many women internalize this view. As such, women's choice to be self-sacrificing may be reinforced by the cultural context.

A rise in the number of women who participate in the labor force is often accompanied by a decline in family size (Hird & Abshoff, 2000; Livingston & Cohn, 2010). This tends to reinforce a stereotype that women who do not have children are career-oriented and have substituted their careers for parenthood. Cameron (1997, as cited in Hird & Abshoff, 2000) has noted that men often view their commitment to their careers as one of their reasons for not having children. Additionally, the men interviewed by Park (2005) were more likely to consider financial consequences of having children.

It is possible that traditional expectations placed upon men to be the family's provider may partly explain why men are more likely to consider the financial impact of having children when deciding not to have children. Men's concerns were primarily related to the idea that having children would restrict their leisure activities, their ability to acquire material wealth, and their ability to maintain their present life style (Park, 2005). By contrast, while some women described concerns about finances, they were more related to economic stability rather than acquiring wealth. They were more likely to voice concerns about whether they would be able to support children's needs and provide financially for their future. For some women interviewed by Callan (1983) (as cited in Hird & Abshoff, 2000), the financial advantages afforded by not having children were seen as a benefit, not a reason to not have children. They voiced the desire to save for retirement or a home, help ageing parents or others, and have extra money to spend on themselves.

Internal Doubts and Regrets

Some research (Delyser, 2011; Morell, 2000) have addressed the issue as to whether women who opt out of motherhood, experience or will, at some point in the future, feel regret regarding their decision to live without children. In addition, although women may report moments of ambivalence, this is not always perceived by them as regret indicative of a strong wish that they had made a different choice or a belief that they had made the 'wrong' choice. According to Morell (2000), who studied the experiences of women who reject motherhood, the women recognized that their decision had resulted in them missing out on some unique pleasures of having children while simultaneously reporting contentment with their choice.

DeLyser (2011) looked at regret in a sample of 15 midlife, married and non-married women who do not have children. The results indicated that the women rarely experienced regret or ambivalence about their decisions. Some of the women reported a fleeting experience of regret, which they felt seemed to emanate mostly in response to others' comments about their choice and, in particular, predictions that they would regret their decision in old age. Most women reported being happy with their decision and stated they had made the right decision. One woman reported, "I have to say that I think it is an erroneous assumption that [childfree] women at midlife are regretful." She further stated, "I don't think of it as sad or regretful. I think of women who have made that decision as having more interesting lives" (DeLyser, 2011, p.68). However, two women in this study of 15 reported being happy with their decision but also voiced some regret. One stated she did not have children and regretted it because her husband is much older than she is and she assumed she would outlive her husband and have no one around to keep her company. The other woman felt regret because she wondered who would visit her when she is in her 60s and 70s. Based on these two women's accounts, it seems that loneliness in old age and concerns regarding ongoing connections or companionship may be a basis for regret for some women.

The language used by women who have chosen not to have children when they discuss their doubt about their normally comfortable choice include "being wistful", having "unsettling rumblings", "musings", "twinges", and "passing thoughts" (Morell, 2000). Some women report that, given the societal messages and pressures to have children, it is almost impossible not to have some moments of ambivalence (DeLyser, 2011; Park, 2005). In Morell's (2000) study, when 34 women who ages 40 and 78 years who had decided not to have children were interviewed after this decision, these women reported that at times they felt isolated as there are not many books or other published works about the experience of childfree women from which they could draw comfort and thus feel and know that they were not alone. Some of these women reported feeling their twinges of doubt or regret in times of loneliness or after they had incurred a loss. For instance, they recognized that if they lost a husband, sibling, or parent, they may long for a distraction or comfort of having someone around. A few of the women recognized that these moments of doubt were associated with concerns as to who would take care of them in time of need or old age.

The decision to live without children is an extremely complex choice. Women who make this decision often hold on to it for years or decades as they attempt to feel secure in it. As such, it is understandable that such a decision would evoke some ambivalence, conflict and doubt that would manifest at different times and in different ways throughout an adult woman's life cycle. For instance, the decision may feel different and mean something different for a woman in her 30s, 50s, and 70s.

Establishing a Feminine Identity Without Motherhood

Social research reveals a strong and positive link between wellbeing and social connectedness. For women, social connection may be particularly related to life satisfaction (Kroll, 2011). This is likely related to societal norms which link women's identity to being caring and nurturing. For some childfree women, activities such as volunteering in areas of human services seem to give them an avenue to affirm their female gender identity (Peterson & Engwall, 2013).

When women without children have been asked to describe their experience of being without children, their responses do not indicate a disturbed feminine identity. Many of these women do not associate femininity with motherhood and tend to reject the notion that foregoing motherhood makes them less of a woman.

According to Morell (2000), who interviewed 34 married women who are intentionally without children ages 40 to 78 years on their experiences of reproductive refusal, she found that being without children supports these women's abilities to be self-determined and to focus on important relationships, creativity, political activism, professional development, leisure activities, which some women have reported to be a direct result of not having children (Morell, 2000).

Peacock (1998), a well-known poet cited in Morell (2000), captured these sentiments in her memoir:

> When I said No to having children, I felt as if I went to some viscerally interior place, the place of recognition. I'd always thought that the positive, the embracing, the Yes that is so characteristic of women's assumed responses, would let me affirm who I am. But it was a refusal that led me to understand my own nature. It was the saving no. The saving no seemed to emerge from the ready emptiness that is required for all creativity, not just for the making of art. That NO can't be confused with loss, or painful emptiness of not having what you need. Like a well-proportioned, unfurnished room with open windows, the affirming refusal invites life. It's a room, not a womb. Like a womb, it harbors life, but unlike a womb, it leaves room to create the rest of life (p.314).

Peacock reversed the meaning of childfreedom and redefined the emptiness as creative growth. For her, absence is reconceptualized as an affirmation for being voluntarily childfree and the concept of childfreedom is seen as a gift, that of possibility and creativity (Morell, 2000).

Gillespie's (2003) and Park's (2005) studies suggest that women without children see advantages of their choice to be related to enhanced freedom, increased opportunities, autonomy, improved financial status, and closer intimate relationships, whereas motherhood is viewed as a burden, sacrifice, duty, loss of identity, and involving demands they are not interesting in taking on.

One woman stated, "when I look at parents and children I think, you have to give so much up. Where are the gains? Why do it?" (Gillespie, 2003, p.130). Another woman reported seeing motherhood as losing her freedom, her identity, and independence. She stated:

> For me, it's almost like being not quite subjugated, but at everyone else's beck and call except your own. I think in part you need to lose your identity as an individual person to cope with looking after children and ferrying them here, there, and everywhere. Very often, your choice about what you want to do, who you are, or what you need is lost. That can go on for 15 to 18 years or even longer" (p.131).

Furthermore, some women perceive having children as resulting in a surrender of the self and a loss of a separate self or identity outside of being a mother. To illustrate this perception, a woman in Gillespie's (2003) study that explores the gender identity of women who are voluntarily childfree reported that:

> [motherhood] conjures up dreariness. … For example, the girls who I meet with at work, it just seems to be one thing after another. All they become is this… child. They become the mother, and the whole of the rest of their personality is just gone. Some girls can't talk about anything else. Trying to talk about something else it's like: I don't know about that or I can't cope with that. (p.132).

Gillespie's (2003) findings suggest that the women's concerns about the loss of their independent identity, was particularly salient for some women.

Coping Mechanisms for Women Without Children

Despite the potential for being ostracized for their choices, women who do not have children also identify sources of support for their decision. Some women reported receiving support from their closest friends and family members. Mueller and Yoder

(1999) found that the most common positive feedback women received was affirmation that they made a good choice or that they made a smart and thoughtful decision; however, this affirmation often came from women who had chosen to have children but who said that they had regretted their families' size or who were envious of their freedom.

Women without children have described a range of ways they have used in order to cope with the negative stereotypes they have faced and to deflect negative remarks made by others about them (Park, 2005). Some women without children in a study by Mueller and Yoder (1999) reported using coping tactics, such as avoiding the topic of family, choosing friends who support their choice, allowing others to assume they are infertile or delaying childbearing, and sometimes lying about their intentions to start a family. Some women stopped associating with people who did not respect their choice.

Some women without children have described additional strategies for support and protection. They have described alternate ways of expressing and satisfying their urge to take care of others, perhaps traditionally conceptualized in gendered ways as a 'maternal urge' in the contexts of a love of animals or through work helping others (Doyle et al., 2015). In addressing the potential challenges of facing old age without children, some women describe reaching agreements with their friends and family to receive care and support. Others have made financial arrangements so that they do not have to rely on others to take care of them.

Summary

The proportion of women who voluntarily and intentionally choose not to have children has been increasing for the past few decades. Despite the increase, these women are still viewed negatively as women's identities continue to be linked with motherhood.

Women who choose not to become mothers may still experience themselves as judged to be deviant, selfish, unwomanly, and immature (McQuillan et al., 2012; Mollen, 2006).

The relatively high rate of voluntarily childfree individuals in the recent decades can in part be attributable to contemporary socio-political and economic factors. Societal changes have made it easier for people to make choices about their reproduction. Enhanced methods of birth control have given women more control over their fertility. The upsurge in the number of women in the paid labor force coupled with the woman's rights movement which has advocated for changes in gender roles have also given women more opportunities and ways to define themselves other than motherhood (Gillespie, 2003). Furthermore, the increased number of women who have sought higher education and delayed marriage is positively correlated with their increased participation in the paid labor force, suggesting that the higher their education level, the more likely women are to delay marriage and children (Craig, Donovan, Fraenkel, Watson, Hawley, & Quinn, 2014).

Moreover, the advent of other social movements that promote freedom of choice, civil liberties, broader definitions of sexual orientation and fertility, and abortion have also contributed to those changes.

The research reviewed in this chapter indicates that women without children are more likely to be White, though the number of women of color who do not have children is increasing significantly (Livingston & Cohn, 2010; Livingston, 2015). Women who do not have children also tend to be highly educated, less religious, and hold managerial or professional positions (Doyle et al., 2015; Livingston & Cohn, 2010). Investigations into the reasons behind women's decisions not to have children indicate an intersection of multiple factors related to concerns related to freedom, academic and career goals, philanthropic concerns, intimacy with partners, rejecting traditional gender roles, early family experiences, anxiety about childbirth, among others (Hird & Abshoff, 2000; Mollen, 2006; Park, 2005).

In relation to how women feel about their decision to not bear children (DeLyser, 2011; Park, 2005), many women have associated this with a sense of positive identity, feeling more able to freely attend to their own needs unlike mothers whom they perceive as sacrificing themselves and being burdened (Morell, 2000). In order to cope with the stigmatization, some women reported keeping their choice a secret, avoiding the topic, or changing their social circle to include people who accept their choice (DeLyser, 2011; Mueller & Yoder, 1999).

Although the research has focused on older childfree women's reasons for being without children and how they have experienced their choice, further research is needed; research aimed at exploring the experience of these women, between the ages of 25 to 40 years, taking into consideration more recent discourses on gender and family life. Given that womanhood was so intimately tied to motherhood in previous generations, the experience of women actively engaged in the process of deciding to remain without children remains under-explored.

Furthermore, the literature indicates that in relation to the decision making process, the type of family origin and social support have been particularly important factors in playing a key role in supporting women who make this decision. Moreover, the research indicates that for some women, the process begins early in life, whereas for others, it evolves over time, after certain life experiences. Still others never directly made a decision (Houseknecht, 1979). It remains important to further understand the

experiences of women who are voluntarily without children's decision as it is currently

happening.

CHAPTER THREE

METHOD

The purpose of this study was to expand upon existing research that has investigated the experience of women who have intentionally chosen not to have children, be it giving birth to children, or being a step-parent or foster parent. While the existing literature contains studies examining the experiences and motives of these women, these studies have focused more on women who had already passed their childbearing years and have not always distinguished between those who are voluntarily without children and those who are involuntarily without children. This study explored the experience of women between the ages of 25 and 40 who have intentionally chosen to be without children.

Participants were asked to discuss how they arrived at their decisions, as well as to reflect on how this decision was related to their sense of self as a woman. Through qualitative interviews, this study attempted to explore the relationship between childfree women's identity or sense of self and the decision not to become mothers.

Research Design

This study used a qualitative, exploratory approach in order to allow the participants to more fully describe their subjective experiences of being without children. Using open-ended questions, participants were asked to reflect on how they arrived at the decision to not have children as well as what effects, if any, their decisions had on their sense of themselves. Data from the interview were analyzed using interpretative phenomenological analysis (IPA) in order to identify themes that emerged from the participants' narratives.

Participants

This study recruited 10 women. Individuals were only eligible to participate in this study after meeting the following conditions:

- Participants must be between the ages of 25 and 40

- Participants must be intentionally without children

  - For the purpose of this study, the term childfree is used to refer to individuals who have decided that they will not bear children or be a parent to a step or foster child.

Participants were not eligible if:

- They desire or intend to have children at a later time in their lives

- They have non-biological children (step-children, or adopted or foster children)

- They are in a state of crisis, are distressed, or were recently hospitalized for mental health issues.

Procedures

Soliciting Participants

Participants who were eligible for the study and met the inclusion criteria were recruited by word-of-mouth, by posting recruitment flyers (Appendix A) at houses of worship, gyms, community centers, health centers, graduate schools, Craigslist, and through the use of FaceBook with a participation solicitation posting (Appendix B). The FaceBook posting included a brief explanation of the study as well as a request to forward the email or share the posting to additional contacts. In addition, a purposive snowball sampling method was used in order to advertise the study through the

researcher's known professional acquaintances.

Enrolling Participants

Participants who were interested in participating in the study were instructed to

contact the researcher through the phone number or email listed on the flyer. During the

initial phone or email conversation, the researcher provided a brief explanation of the

study as well as the expected time commitment and compensation it involved. When

subjects expressed interest, the researcher screened them to ensure that they met all

inclusion and exclusion criteria prior to arranging the interview and mailed them a

demographic questionnaire (see Appendix C) with a stamped return envelope. Prior to

mailing the demographic questionnaire, the researcher created pseudonyms for each

participant in order to ensure the anonymity of the information they provide. These

pseudonyms were used for each interviewed participant. Identifying pseudonyms were

stored on the researcher's password protected encrypted computer stored in the

researcher's home. Once the demographic questionnaires were mailed back, participants

were contacted by their preferred method to schedule an interview date either in person or

via Skype. Participants were reminded that the interview would ask personal questions

and be audio-recorded using two digital recorders in case one became defected and would

be transcribed later by the researcher without their identifying information, and that they

could choose not to answer any questions or stop the interview at any time without any

consequence. They were also informed that the audio records and transcriptions would

be destroyed seven years after the study was completed per research study protocol.

Subjects who agreed to participate scheduled a meeting with the researcher at a mutually agreed private location to meet for the approximately hour-long face-to-face interview or via Skype and would be compensated a $30 visa giftcard for their participation even if they decided to withdraw at any time. For participants who selected to do the interview via Skype, two copies of the Informed Consent form were mailed to them immediately with a return stamped envelope prior to their interview date. This allowed them to manually sign a copy and mail it back to the researcher prior to their interview as well as enabled them to retain a copy of the consent form. The form was discussed at the beginning of the interview in order to ensure full understanding of the document. After the Skype interviews, participants were mailed a $30 gift card for their participation. Subjects who wanted to participate in the study but were not eligible were thanked for their interest and informed that they could not be selected. During the scheduled meeting, subjects were greeted and provided with an Informed Consent Form (see Appendix D). Once the participants read and signed the Informed Consent Form, and the researcher answered any questions the participants had, the interview began. In the event that participants experienced discomfort or adverse effects during or after the interview, they were provided a list of referral sources; however, none of the participants reported discomfort during or after the interviews were conducted.

Data Collection

As mentioned above, this study aimed to use a qualitative approach, using a demographic questionnaire and pre-formulated semi-structured interview questions to guide the interview and encourage participant description of their experiences. Please refer to Appendix E for a list of questions and possible follow-up questions. These questions were designed to facilitate the respondents' exploration of their subjective experiences of being without children as well as the factors that they reported as having

contributed to their choice.

Data Storage

The audio-recorded data gathered from the interview questions were stored in an

encrypted and password-protected computer and the written transcriptions by the

researcher were kept in a locked and secured location in the researcher's home. All

participants' information were de-identified or disguised in order to protect their

confidentiality. Upon completion of the study, per research study protocol, all audiofiles

and materials with identified information were kept confidentially and will be destroyed

after seven years.

Debriefing of Participants

After the completion of each interview, the researcher allowed a 10-minute

debriefing period (see Appendix F) for any questions or concerns that surfaced during the

interview. Although this study was considered of minimal risk to participants, the

subjects were provided the researcher's contact information in case any questions or

concerns arose afterward. In the event that a participant experienced adverse effects

during or after the interview, the researcher made herself available to offer support and

provided a list of referrals (see Appendix G) if the participant desired to seek additional

care. None of the participants reported adverse effects after the interviews were

conducted.

Protection of Participants/Ethical Considerations

In order to ensure that participants were protected and not distressed by the

interview experience, certain precautions were taken. For example, subjects were

59

informed that they could terminate the interview at any time for any reason without any consequences even after providing their informed consent. If a participant withdrew consent, any data already collected would not be used and would be destroyed immediately. None of the participants terminated the interview prematurely.

The researcher provided as many breaks as needed to participants during the interview process to assure their well-being; however, none of them required it. The researcher did not withhold any information regarding detailed information about the study and the participants' right both verbally and through the Informed Consent Form (see Appendix D) and the Debriefing Statement (see Appendix F). Finally, the researcher had the study reviewed and approved by the administrative Institutional Review Board at William James College before potential participants could be recruited in an effort to ensure that the study met all of the guidelines in the Ethical Principles of Psychologists and Code of Conduct of the American Psychological Association.

Data Analysis

The data obtained from the semi-structured interviews were analyzed and coded for key themes using interpretive phenomenological analysis (IPA). IPA is a method used to understand participants' lived experiences as well as how they make sense of their experiences (Smith, Flowers, & Larkin, 2009). Using this method, researchers reflect upon their own preconceptions or bias about the data and attempt to suppress them in order to focus on understanding the experiential world of the participants. Transcripts are coded in detail, focusing on key claims made by the participants based on the researcher's interpretation of their meaning. As the analysis develops, the researcher groups similar codes together to begin to identify themes and patterns which are then summarized. As such, this method specifically attempted to understand the meanings

that participants attach to their own experience. The data was shared with the

researcher's committee for additional analysis and examination. This analysis was used

to explore the factors that contributed to the women's decision to be without children as

well as to explore their decision-making process and the resulting effects the decision had

on their sense of self. The themes identified were used to describe the women's

experiences as well as to discern similarities and differences across their experiences.

CHAPTER FOUR

RESULTS

This chapter presents the findings of this study. The main purpose of the study was to explore and understand the experience and decision-process of women who choose to be without children as well as any impact this decision may have had on their sense of self. The goal of this study was to explore specifically the experiences of women born after the second wave of feminism. The results of these interviews will begin with information on the participants' demographic data, followed by short biographical sketches of each participant. Next, a thematic analysis uncovering themes in the experiences of participants will be discussed using pseudonyms to refer to them in order to maintain their anonymity. Quotes from the interviews will be used throughout the analysis in order to illustrate these different themes. Finally, this chapter will conclude with a summary of the results.

Participant Demographics

A total of 10 women participated in the study (see Table 1). Nine of the interviews were performed in person and one was performed via Skype. Ages of the participants ranged between 26 and 40 years old. Seven participants identified their ethnicity as White; two participants identified as Asian; and one as African American. Participants' religion varied: one participant identified as being Agnostic; one identified as Atheist; two identified as Spiritual, with one of them being non-religious; two identified as having no religion, however, one was raised Catholic; one identified as Buddhist; one identified as having three religions: Islam, Catholicism, and Buddhism; one identified as a liberal Christian; and one as Roman Catholic. Of the ten participants,

62

nine identified as being straight and one as bisexual. Highest education levels ranged from General Educational Development (GED) to graduate degree. One participant reported having a GED; four reported a college degree, with one of them currently enrolled in a master's program and the other one in a doctoral program; five participants reported having a graduate degree. It is important to note that four of the participants who selected graduate degree as their highest level of education were currently enrolled in graduate school and one was currently doing her post-doctoral internship. Also of importance is that four out of the ten participants were students of psychology.

Participants were also asked to provide information about their relationship status. Five participants identified as being single, two as being married, and three as living together with their partners, with one engaged to be married in the summer of the current year, and one currently living in a different city as her partner.

Table 1. Participant Demographic Data

Number of Participants		N=10
Age Range	25 – 30 years	N=3
	31 – 35 years	N=4
	36 – 40 years	N=3
Race and/or Ethnicity	White	N=7
	Black	N=1
	Asian	N=2
Religion	Agnostic	N=1
	Atheist	N=1
	Catholic	N=1
	None	N=2 (1 raised Catholic)
	Spiritual	N=2 (1 Non-Religious)
	Liberal Christian	N=1
	Buddhism	N=1
	Islam, Catholicism, Buddhism	N=1
Sexual Orientation	Straight	N=9
	Bisexual	N=1
Highest Level of Education	GED	N=1
	College	N=4 (2 in a graduate program)
	Graduate Degree	N=5 (1 post-doctoral)

Table 1. (Cont.)

Number of Participants		N=10
Relationship Status	Single	N=5
	Married	N=2
	Living together	N=3 (1 engaged to be married in a few months)

Biographical Sketches

Hayley is a 32 year old, White woman, who is currently doing her post-doctoral internship in Psychology. She identifies as a straight woman who lives with her boyfriend; however, they are currently living in separate cities until she finishes her internship. While she was raised Catholic, she does not identify as being a member of any religious groups.

Phoebe is a 27 year old, single African American woman who identifies as being bisexual. She identifies as being Spiritual. Her highest education level is GED.

Kayla is a 39 year old White married woman. She identifies as being straight and is Roman Catholic. Her highest education level is four years of college.

Wendy is a 40 year old, single Asian woman who identifies as being straight. She dated a man for a long time and became pregnant by him but had a miscarriage just months before her boyfriend passed from cancer. Her highest education level is a graduate degree, she works as an accountant, and she is currently enrolled in a doctoral program. She identifies Islam, Catholicism, and Buddhism as her religions.

Abigail is a 33 year old, straight White woman who lives with her fiancé and is engaged to be married in the summer of this year. She identifies as being non-religious Spiritual. Her highest education level is a graduate degree and is currently enrolled in a doctoral program in Psychology.

Theresa is a 39 year old, single, straight, White woman. She identifies as being a liberal Christian. Her highest education level is a graduate degree from Library school.

Carol is a 27 year old, single, straight, Asian woman. She identifies Buddhism as her religion. Her highest education level is four years of college; however, she is currently enrolled in a master's program in Psychology.

Aria is a 35 year old, straight, White, married woman. She does not belong to any religious groups. Her highest education level is four years of college.

Erin is a 26 year old, single, straight, White woman. She identifies as being agnostic. Her highest education level is a graduate degree and is currently enrolled in a doctoral program in Psychology.

Brandy is a 33 year old, straight, White woman who lives with her partner. She identifies as an atheist. Her highest education level is four years of college; however, she is currently enrolled in a doctoral program in Psychology.

Table 2. Participant Quick Reference Data

Participant	Age	Race and/or Ethnicity	Religion	Sexual Orientation	Highest Education Level	Relation-ship Status
Hayley	32	White	Raised Catholic now None	Straight	Graduate degree in Psychology doing her post-doctoral internship	Living with her partner but currently in separate cities
Phoebe	27	African American	Spiritual	Bisexual	GED	Single
Kayla	39	White	Roman Catholic	Straight	College degree	Married
Wendy	40	Asian	Islam,Catholi cism , Buddhism	Straight	Graduate degree, enrolled in a doctoral program	Single

Table 2 (Cont.)

Participant	Age	Race and/or Ethnicity	Religion	Sexual Orientation	Highest Education Level	Relation-ship Status
Abigail	33	White	Non-Religious Spiritual	Straight	Graduate degree, enrolled in a doctoral program in Psychology	Engaged to be married in the summer of this year
Theresa	39	White	Liberal Christian	Straight	Graduate degree in Library	Single
Carol	27	Asian	Buddhism	Straight	College degree and currently enrolled in a master's program in Psychology	Single
Aria	35	White	None	Straight	College degree	Married
Erin	26	White	Agnostic	Straight	Graduate degree and currently enrolled in a doctoral program in Psychology	Single
Brandy	33	White	Atheist	Straight	College degree and currently enrolled in a doctoral program in Psychology	Living with partner

Main Results

This qualitative study used a semi-structured interview process in which 10

women participated. The participants were asked nine main questions with follow-up

questions in order to encourage them to elaborate more on their answers (see Appendix

A). The interviews lasted from 15 to 64 minutes; however, on average, most interviews took about 22 minutes to complete. Each interview was audio-recorded and later transcribed by the interviewer-researcher. Upon completion of all ten transcripts, the researcher used a thematic analysis when reading them in order to uncover any themes that may have been present in the participants' experiences of being without children.

In carefully reading the transcripts, several important findings emerged about the participants' experiences of choosing not to have children. These findings will be discussed in detail, including how the participants arrived at the decision to not have children or their decision-process, and any factors that may have led to or influenced their decision. Further, the participants' reflections on their experiences of being without children as well as the impact the decision may have had on their sense of self will be explored. Lastly, their thoughts about how they may feel about their decision in the future will be discussed.

Participants' Discovery of Their Choice to not Have Children

While some participants reported their choice to not have children as a process, the majority stated they did not necessarily make a decision. Several participants had difficulty recalling how they came to decide. They described the experience as "just knowing" but reported not having thought about the idea of having children until their first romantic relationship as a teenager or their first committed relationship as an adult. Others said they did not think about it until their friends mentioned it.

Not Remembering Ever Wanting Children

Nine out of ten participants reported not remembering that they ever wanted children. They described their experience as "always knowing", "lacking the desire" or the "maternal instinct" to become a mother. For example, Hayley, 32, explained,

I think, even from somewhat of an early age, like 13 years old, I don't remember ever wanting to have children…because that's sort of like high school, when you start to have relationships and things like that, and I guess I never really envisioned my life being like that, with kids, whereas my other friends would talk about wanting to have kids. I never felt like I wanted that life.

Hayley explained further that she never felt the desire to have children. She said "other people seem to desperately want to have children, and they just really want to be a mom, and I have never, I never feel like that".

Seven participants recalled the thought of not having children occurring in their teenage years. Kayla, 39, recounted that "it wasn't necessarily a decision. It was something I've just always known… it [is] the lack of truly wanting that experience… I've never wanted that." Similarly, Theresa, 39, said,

I've never had that maternal instinct. Several of my friends, I mean, I've heard, 'Oh, I've always wanted children'. I've never wanted children. It's, I don't know what it was.

Two individuals reported knowing since childhood. For instance, Erin, 26, stated,

I don't know if there was a specific time when I decided that I didn't want kids; it was just sort of always something I've known. I remember being a kid and not liking other kids. Like, I'm not the warmest and fuzziest of people, so I just like, I just never felt the need to have kids.

Aria, 35, said she "knew, probably as a teenager. I kind of like, knew." Brandy, 33, also expressed knowing since childhood. She said,

"So I actually always knew that I didn't wanna have children even when I was a child. So as far back as I can remember, I, I played with dolls and I really liked taking care of my dolls and you know, I had Barbies and I played house. But my Barbie and my Ken never had children."

Although most participants felt the process was implicit or gradual, in contrast, one participant, Phoebe, 27, reported that her decision also occurred in her teenage year, and described it as a "snap decision." She provided a specific reason and disclosed that she was abused as a child and would not want anyone else to have that experience. She said,

> It's like that kind of Southern domestic abuse that kind of seems normalized in our culture, so I just, I wouldn't put anybody else through that, so I don't want to have kids.

She further expounded, "seeing all these people made all these same mistakes and mistreat their children… and using them to manipulate [others]…, having children just seemed like an irresponsible thing to do."

Though the participants were comfortable with their choice and expressed not wanting the lifestyle of being a parent, some linked their choice to lacking a "maternal instinct". This indicates an awareness that their choice is not considered the norm, but somehow, the impact of the larger culture still affected the way they view their choice or themselves.

Realization Made Over Time

Even though most participants reported knowing since childhood or their teenage years that they did not want to have children, one participant said she did not know until she was in college. Carol, 27, recalled her decision process,

> I kind of slowly came to a decision. It kind of dawned on me as I got older, I guess… But as I grew older, I came to see that, yeah, this is no joke… I can say as I started working, so maybe in my twenties, like, 20 to 23.

Vacillating on the Thought of not Having Children

Though the majority of the participants reported not necessarily making a decision about not having children, six recalled having moments when they wavered and wondered whether or not they were making the right choice. For example, Abigail, 33, explained,

My friends were all getting married and having children in their twenties and I'm
in my thirties and I'm just getting married now. There was a point where
everyone around me was getting married and having kids. I was like, 'Oh my
gosh, this is it. This is the breaking point where everyone else is going to go off
in that direction and I'm going to go off here'. I felt a little stress about that, like
maybe I'm making the wrong decision.

These participants also reported that they "always went back to 'No, this is the
right choice for me'." For instance, Hayley, 32, also recalled questioning her choice,

There definitely has been times in my life where I, you know, seriously
considered it, and thought about [having children], you know, what would happen
if I did… and every time I think about it, I just think that, that is just not me. I
just don't see myself as a mom.

Others stated they did not question their choice. For example, Erin, 26, said "it
was just sort of always something I've known. I just never felt the need to have kids."

Kayla, 39, explained that "knowing in my heart that it just wasn't something I
truly wanted". She further expounded, "I've never actually wavered. I've never actually
had this moment or space of time where I was like 'you know what, maybe, you know."

It wasn't a professional issue like I don't have time to have kids or that I want to
travel around the world, you know. Kids just won't do. …For me, that was, uh,
you know, it's something I've just never wavered on. For the longest time, I
waited. I thought, 'something, maybe something will come over me', but it
didn't.

What Made the Decision Easy or Difficult

Response of family. Participants talked about their decision process in terms of
what made it easier or harder to decide. Some referenced family and societal "pressure",
others mentioned doing some "soul-searching".

Seven participants reported feeling pressure from family, specifically their
mothers, as something that made them question their choice or made it harder to feel

settled in their choice. For instance, Theresa, 39, said "if I was to say what made it

harder, my mother really wants to be a grandmother." Similarly, Erin, 26, said,

> Something that made it harder to decide is that I have gotten pressure from my
> family, like, you know, the typical families, 'Oh, when are you having kids?' that
> sort of question. My mother really pressured me for a while and she sort of, I've
> talked to her about it and she's sort of at the point now where she recognizes that I
> don't want it. I think she still thinks I'll change my mind, but definitely family
> pressure has made it hard and having to have that conversation with multiple
> people on multiple occasions, because I say, 'Oh' and start laughing and they're
> like, 'No, but really, when are you having kids?' and I'm like 'I don't know, it's
> not in my plan', so that can, that's definitely hard.

> Kayla, 39, expressed similar sentiments,

> Parental pressure, from my mother, made it harder. It's like that expression 'I'm
> not upset with you, I'm just disappointed'. It's like, okay, put a knife through my
> heart right now. I'd rather you be mad and pissed than disappointed. And my
> mom would say things like 'Oh, you'd have such beautiful children, you have
> such a way with kids'. Because oddly enough, for years, I actually worked in
> private school admissions with young children. I was with them all the time.
> And it was, for me it was like, 'Yeah, yep, yeah'. Every day, reaffirming where I
> was. I'm like, 'Uh huh, that's, I'm good, I'm good'.

Wendy, a 40 year old graduate student, experienced the same "pressure" from her

family to have children; however, she explained what made it more difficult to make that

choice is her love for children, most specifically her anxiety for their well-being. She

said that if she had children, her "life would be all about her children" and that she would

be afraid "for them to even leave the house". She explained that she can be very

protective and feared that that "would make them unhappy." Brandy, 33, said her mother

was "very upset" and took a long time "to come to terms with her decision, which created

"a bone of contention" between them. She expressed that she is "very teary" when her

mother says, "'I know I'm not gonna have any grandchildren'". She also reported getting

frustrated when her mother occasionally asks who will take care of her in her old age.

Brandy stated that she is not the one taking care of her mother and that she hopes her mother did not have her "thinking that that was sort of the end result 'cause there's no guarantees to those types of things, like you can't predict any of that".

In contrast to what most participants reported, three stated they did not feel the "pressure". Phoebe, 27, explained,

> I think it was a very neutral decision really… I wasn't feeling the weight of the world on my shoulders…so there was nothing behind [her decision] to make it difficult or easy.

Similarly, Aria, 35, stated "I don't let people influence my reproductive choice, ever, because it's my own choice." Likewise, Brandy, 33, said,

> I don't think there is anything that made [deciding] hard. It's never been a temptation or desire. I don't feel, like a gut reaction that a lot of women seem to, I don't wanna generalize them, but women who talk about wanting to have children, they talk about this longing inside of them. Almost like an ache. I have never had that.

In terms of what made their choice easier, six participants talked about knowing they did not want to have children. For example, Kayla, 39, said "what made it easier was knowing in my heart that it just wasn't something I truly wanted". Some mentioned their lack of desire, their background with trauma, or growing up poor. Others talked about seeing the experience of others who have children that made their decision easier.

Carol, 27, talked about not having "a good role model" to become a parent and not wanting to be "burdensome".

Soul-searching and self-evaluation. Four participants reported "soul-searching" and "self-evaluation" as playing a role in finalizing their decision to not have children. Wendy, 40, reported feeling thankful after her miscarriage because she did not want to have a child, but her religion helped her to feel "calm" and "at peace" with herself. She said in hindsight, she felt her now deceased partner should not have asked her to have his child "so [he] could remind him or her as me" when he discovered he had a few months to live. She added that it "scared" her because she doesn't believe children should serve as "memory". She explained,

> … it's like you build the mind or the principle to this human being to be, you know, another person that can be good for others, not for replacing you. That's what the statement, I don't like that statement.

Similarly, Carol, 27, reported listening to a Buddhist preacher on YouTube, which has been helpful in dealing with her family issues as well as her decision to not have children. She said,

> So it kind of, like, gradually dawned on me that like, a) I should never have kids, b) I might adopt, maybe, but no. For now. So I guess I kind of, like, formed that kind of thought, kind of crystallized in my head. But I'm, like, really, really hoping that I don't change my mind.

Carol said she is so worried about changing her mind later that she has thought about having a hysterectomy as a "preventative medicine". Abigail, 33, reported feeling a lot of "social pressure" to have children. She said after doing "a little soul searching", practicing "some mindfulness", and doing what she does for "self-care", she gave herself "permission to feel that divergence from, kind of, the societal norm." She added, "from that point on, I've really said I don't want to". Likewise, Theresa, 39, expressed being part of a group called "adult children of dysfunctional families", which has been helpful in teaching her to look within herself, and to take care of herself and her needs. She said, "as I've developed more self-knowledge, I've been less thrilled with the idea of connect". She explained that she is more interested in taking care of herself than connecting with another human being, which she described as "draining". She also referenced her recovery process in a 12-step program as being "very eye-opening". She said,

There, there's a process of looking at the lies you tell yourself. One of the lies was, like, I'm only a woman fulfilled if I have children. And then the truth in that, the truth side of the lie is no one completely, like, I'm a completely, whole, person regardless of, it's like it's what they call misplaced values. I had to come to terms with the fact that I do not [want to be a mother], I have no desire to be that, that person right now.

Impact of Romantic Relationship on Choice

At the time of the interview, several participants mentioned their relationship status and talked about it in relation to their decision process. Others reflected on their experience of choosing not to have children while in a relationship with a partner who is indifferent about having children. Five participants reported being single, one was engaged, two were married, and two were in a committed relationship and living with their significant other. Of the five single participants, two reported not being interested in having or pursuing romantic relationships. Phoebe, 27, said, "I don't partake in [romantic relationships]."

Eight participants reported that being in a relationship has not, does not, or would not change the way they feel about their decision. Several stated it would be a "deal breaker" if their partner or the person they are dating wants to have children. For example, Kayla, 39, said "it would be a problem if my husband wanted to have children.., so thank God, we are in alignment, so we're good…. It would be a deal breaker if we weren't." Wendy, 40, struggled with letting her decision be known at the start of a relationship or as the relationship develops. When asked whether or not she thinks that would have an effect on her decision, she said, "If he really loves me and he's still pushing it, I would just walk away." Theresa, 39, said she has not been with any man who wants children. Similarly, Carol, 27, said, "I guess it definitely helps that the person I'm seeing, I mean, he, I mean, we are on the same page." Likewise, Aria, 35, said, "there's really no push from him to get pregnant, and I just don't really see it happening. It's probably, like, a 99% chance that's not going to happen, ever." Erin, 26, said she has dated men in the past who wanted to have children, and she noted that it was a "deal breaker" for her because she had to end several relationships. She added that she is adamant about her decision and she does not foresee it changing.

Brandy, 33, expressed similar sentiments. She shared that she is thankful that she is in a relationship with a man who feels the same way because this "issue" has impacted previous romantic relationships as "it closes the door." She also indicated that if she were no longer with her significant other, the first thing she would tell people when she meets them is that she does not want to have children. She explained,

> I'd be like, 'well, just so you know, like this is an important thing that you should know'. And I could imagine people, you know, saying like, 'Oh, I was really hoping to have children' or 'Oh, I already have one from a previous marriage'. That's a deal breaker too. Like, I don't want to be responsible for any children.

Despite "always knowing" she did not want to have children, Hayley, 32, reported including her partner in the decision. She said, "We've been together since I was 19, and so he's definitely been, like, a part of this decision." Kayla, 39, said in regards to including her husband in her decision,

> It was never a heart to heart that we had to have, thank goodness, it was just kinda like, 'Is that where you're at? That's where I'm at. Okay, good'.

Others worried that their partners would change their mind in the future and resent them for not wanting to have children. As such, they described "checking in" occasionally with them to ensure they were in alignment. All women who were either married, engaged, or in a committed relationship (five participants) said these check-ins were prompted by either seeing a couple with children or by being asked when or whether or not they were having children. For example, Hayley, 32, talked about her partner, in the recent months, having "moments" where he questions their decision and wonders, "'Like, what are we going to do with the time that we would be with children.'" She explained that her partner vacillates on the issue, which is concerning to her because she is worried that he might change his mind in the future, "when it actually is too late for me, for that to be a possibility".

Abigail, 33, talked about telling her fiancé about her previous pregnancies and his reaction to it. She explained that they had already discussed her choice and decision, which they were both in agreement on; however, "he's that on the fence guy." She stated that she believes "he'd be okay with one kid" but explained that when he thinks back to being abandoned by his father, he quickly realizes that he does not want to have children, or maybe he does. His indecision in turns, affirms Abigail's decision, and her reaction is "woah, you don't know if you'd leave me if we had a kid, okay, we're not having kids." She described single motherhood as her "worst nightmare" and stated she would not put herself or her child "in that situation". Abigail also talked about not wanting to hurt her fiancé with her decision but also being realistic about all aspects of having children, not just the superficial, as in "seeing a cute baby on the train." She also described these communications as "really important and empowering." She said,

> The last thing I want to do is hurt the person I'm choosing to spend my life with by denying him something so it's just been a constant evaluative process of 'Are we on the same page, are we on the same page, are we on the same page', every 3 to 6 months. Every 3 to 6 months, 'still doing okay?' and I'll put it out there in a non-confusing way, like, "I still don't want kids, how are you feeling about that?' And then every once in a while we'll do it in a playful way. It's kind of a friendly, affectionate way of checking in. And every time we have that reality check, we come back to 'oh, right, we don't want kids.'

This section will present data on what the participants considered as factors leading to their decision to not have children. Participants' responses varied and their views about motherhood were diverse.

Several participants talked about their reasons for choosing not to have children. Though some had difficulty pinpointing exactly which factors contributed to their decision, several of them seemed to have an inkling and listed a combination of things and experiences that they thought may have shaped their choice. Following is a detailed account of what factors led the participants in choosing not to have children.

Background/ Experiences of Being a Child

The experience of being a child or being in one's family was reported as one of the themes in the factors that impacted some of the participants' decision. Two participants reported being emotionally abused by their family of origin or being around an environment in which domestic abuse was "normalized". For example, Phoebe, 27, said she was "abused as a child" and "wouldn't put anybody else through that." Similarly, Carol, 27, explained that she grew up with a "manipulative and abusive" family.

Three participants mentioned growing up around other children in their families as a factor in their decision. For instance, Wendy, 40, reported that her mother housed several of her cousins because they came from a "broken home, family"; as such, she grew up with several other children. She said, "I think that's one of the reasons too, make me make this decision." Theresa, 39, expressed similar sentiments. She explained as one of the main reasons for her decision is that her mother had an "in-home child care", while she was high school, which she was asked to help with. She reported seeing "firsthand how much energy taking care of children is", especially given her mother is a single mother.

Brandy, 33, also talked about her background not predisposing her to want to have children. She referenced seeing others who have children "struggle". She said,

> My background made it really easy to look at the situation and say like, listen, unless you really want children, bringing a child into this world, is uh, ah, awful. It's harmful, potentially, you know, it has lifelong consequences. And so my background, having that exposure and that experience in seeing people who treated children very poorly and people who were in abject poverty, um, trying to raise children. And, their struggle, that made it really easy.

Brandy further explained that she "equated unwanted children and poverty and lifelong trauma and awful things".

Mother's Identification with Being a "Mom"

Three participants referenced their mother's desire to have children as a factor in influencing their choice to not have children. For instance, Kayla, 39, reported that her mother has always wanted to have children and would often say "'I was born to be a mother'". She said, "That's what identified her as a person". She added,

> I never identified myself in the same way… I don't think she ever recovered from us leaving home. It was like she never gained back a sense of who she was because even before she was a mother, she knew she wanted to be a mother. It was like, 'This is, this is my path', and for me, I've never wanted that… We were what identified her, and how I didn't want that.

Brandy, 33, said her mother's a "mom's mom, like she just loves kids" and would have "10 kids if she could". She said she does not want to be like that. Similarly, Theresa, 39, referred to her mother as being "pretty emotionally dependent" and said she recently started "separating a little bit from that emotional dependence".

Doubts About Ability to Manage Parenting

Eight participants alluded to feeling doubtful about their ability to parent resulting from witnessing the impact of others' poor parenting. For example, Aria, 35, recalled being exposed to children working as a Child Welfare Case Manager in the state system and seeing "all the problems that come with that". She said "I guess that job kind of helped put the nail in the coffin about having kids". She added, "you could really do so many things to screw them up, and I just really don't want to even deal with it." Aria also reported babysitting and helping to take care of her younger siblings as a teenager while her parents were at work or away for the weekend. She said, her mother called it "the 'built-in babysitter'". She explained that she "got sick of that responsibility" and said, "I wasn't really allowed to go out and have fun, and we were Catholic, and, you know, I had to stay home and help a lot". Similarly, Wendy, 40, said "it's not easy to be a parent". She was also concerned about how the child would turn out. She said, "Hopefully the kid will grow up just the right way". She added that she gets nervous around children because she worries about their well-being constantly. She said, "I have to be independent... I just want to be comfortable".

Theresa, 39, referred to herself and her family. She said,

> Part of that was looking at my family of origin. It was just looking at a lot of how I got to where I got to, ..., I really don't want to cause anyone to suffer the way I suffered, period.

Theresa further explained that she saw firsthand how much energy taking care of children is. She added that she is an "introvert"; as such, the longer she is around people, the faster her "battery is drained" because she needs time to herself to recharge, "in order to be positively with other people". Theresa also explained that she has had some episodes with depression and has difficulty "planning ahead". She said, "I can't count on, like, being there for someone, like, especially a small child that's like a sponge for energy". She explained that when she helped her mother with her in-home childcare, it "drained" her. She also reported feeling "worn out" after she Facetimes with her niece, which then "reaffirms" her decision not to have children.

Phoebe, 27, said having been abused as a child and looking at her environment, "having children just seemed like an irresponsible thing to do because of the choices that others around me were making." She added that seeing others "make all these same mistakes and mistreat their children" solidified her decision. Carol, 27, said her decision solidified when she started working with children in a psychiatry department as a research assistant in dealing with "parental issues that goes into the child." She also referred to her family of origin and added that she realized her parents are human beings and "did their best, and then, look how I turned out, blah, yeah, I deal with that too". She explained that she struggles with "dysthymia, major depression reoccurring moderate to severe, or nothing at all", something she would not want for her child. She further expounded that working as a residential counselor exposed her to "all this, like, variety of things, dimensions, that makes a child a human", which is when she realized how much "patience, and then, perseverance, and then, firmness" it requires, which she said she lacks. Carol also referred to her "aversion to forging any deep relationship of any kind". She expressed that she has a "phobia of making any deep, personal relationships", which could impact her parenting ability. Similarly, Erin, 26, stated, "I'm not great at like, with needy personalities". She said she would rather not have to deal with "the idea of taking care of somebody". Hayley, 32, said, she did not remember any "specific event or anything like that that happened" but she "babysat a lot" as a teenager and said, "maybe that had an impact". She added that while she babysits her friend's baby occasionally, whom she "loves" and finds "adorable", she also likes to "give her back" because when the baby cries, she said, "it really stresses me out."

Abigail, 33, talked about not wanting the responsibility of having children. She said, "The responsibility of or the idea of having kids just didn't click for me…". She added,

> Just the vulnerability of kids terrifies me. The idea of having a child, and I've seen my ex's mother… go through the grief of seeing him as a substance abuser… And then watching her lose her son… So I think I'm built more as a helper than as someone to actually bear that sort of pain directly. I can bear different kinds of pain.

Abigail also reported that her and her fiancé have a puppy, which is "as far as [she] can go". She said she brings her puppy to her sister's house sometimes and stated "because I can't handle the puppy needing me all the time in the house." She said, "It's a responsibility that I'm just not very good at".

Impact on Career

Seven participants reported that having children would limit their career opportunities or "get in the way" of their plans. Some talked about having aspirations other than making children. For example, Wendy, 40, an accountant and doctoral student, recalled growing up with an older step-sister who became pregnant in her high school years. She explained that her cousin is the only one in the family who did not further her education "cause she start having children". She added that all her female friends who have children "are just like housewife", something she would not want to do. Wendy also referenced the difficulty of having a successful career and children. She shared that she works "a lot" and does not have time for kids; she said, "'cause one or the other, cannot be together two, you know what I mean? So that also makes part of my decision."

Similarly, Erin, 26, talked about a cousin who became pregnant at a young age missing out on opportunities. She said, "something that actually made [her decision] easy was my cousin had a kid at a very young age". She added,

> My cousin missed out on a lot of opportunities from having her kid and she doesn't regret the decision at all but it's sort of, like, there's so many things she could have done that she wanted to do but never had the chance to do. So, for me, I often think about that and I can do these things, if I choose to… I like having all these opportunities available to me.

Erin further explained "even in my work life, like, I prefer to work with adults. Like, I don't know, I just don't do great with kids". Erin added, "education is, like, really important to me". She expressed that if she had taken time off and "settled down and had kids", she would not have gone to graduate school. She said, "This is ultimately the route that I think is best for me". Erin also shared that she worried she would not be an effective parent having to balance a career as a psychologist, which she considers "intense" with "the demands of having kids". She added, "I don't think that would be very good for my mental health".

Hayley, 32, said she has been working towards her career for a long time and "never though it would be possible to do both". She referred to the difficulty of having a career in academia and having children and said,

> … there's been a lot of discourse about this, about women self-selecting out of academia because having children is kind of frowned upon, and it's really difficult to keep this career and have children.

Hayley also explained that she may have had a different perspective if she had chosen a different career path, "like a nurse, a teacher, or something like that", a career in which she could have finished at a younger age that would have allowed her more time to settle into her career before having children; however, she said "that's not my experience, and, maybe my life would be different". Hayley also talked about her other friends without children whose careers are also in academia. She said though they talk about possibly having children, they say they do not know "how or when that will ever happen" because they know it would halt or affect their career. Hayley added, "I chose to go to graduate school", which she considers "a lot of work in and of itself". She also said it's "very important to me to have a successful career, and I feel like the career is more important to me". Hayley, 32, also referenced "dominant discourse" and societal gender roles. She reported only seeing "the negative parts of it." She further expounded, "and even, like, right from the beginning, like, even from the moment of, like, getting pregnant, I just feel like it's all negative." Interestingly, she also said, "if I could be the dad, I would probably feel differently, but being the mom is not appealing to me at all." She added,

> From the moment, you know, like, I'm the one who has to be pregnant. I'm the one whose career is going to be affected. I'm the one who has to breast feed, and the one who has to go back to work after 6 weeks or whatever, and then pump at work. And then when they're sick, they, you know, they're going to call for their mom, they're not going to, you know, they're not going to call for dad. I just, I feel like being the mom is the stressful part and being the dad is the fun part. And if I could be the dad, I maybe would feel differently about this whole situation.

Hayley said that she knows that "dads are important, but they're different". She said, "in the culture and world we're living in, unfortunately, most of the time the onus falls on the mother to do everything."

Aria, 35, also said that she and her husband work a lot and they "don't have time for kids". She said that even as a child, she knew she did not want to have children. She said at the time, she thought, "even when I'm able enough and old enough, I just, just want to get my master's degree and just work, and save my money". Brandy, 33, a performer and a doctoral student, referred to her career as being incompatible with having children as in addition to being a psychologist-in-training, she is a performer and prefers the night-life lifestyle; as such, her "non-traditional schedule and lifestyle don't work for children". Brandy, also said "having a kid would get in the way" of her career, which is very important to her.

Abigail, 33, a school psychologist-in-training, expressed her concerns with her schema of "what a mother should be with what our society's mothering role is." She believes that two-parent working households are "extremely stressful for children" and questions the stability of society. She referred to the "imbalance between the demands that women have on career and child-rearing" which is not yet "balanced by men and their professional and parental roles". She said, "If I were to become a mother, I would have to do my best to fill my own schema of a mother". She stated, "That would take away the attention to the kids that I'm serving now". She explained,

> I would have to put that attention whole heartedly into my child and so it just doesn't, those two don't fit together, so the career versus parent, I just don't feel like I'd be able to do both perfectly well. And so, I've chosen to do one and help the global community at the sacrifice of my own personal community, I guess.

Abigail also said that she would rather help "other kids out and foster kids" if she were to become a parent than "actually procreate" because she does not "know how to meet society's expectations anymore". She added that society expects women to be "a super woman all the time". She said, "I think it's just totally fragmented. There's no clear expectation of anything or role definition". Abigail added,

> I had different aspirations in my career and relationships, and so even throughout my relationships with different significant others, you know, I've always talked to them about having kids and made it very clear that I didn't want to.

Phoebe, 27, travels frequently for her work, and explained that "even when I get off the road, there are still things that I want to do… a kid will really get in the way".

Not Wanting to Meet the Demands of Parenting

Seven participants reported not wanting to meet "other's needs" or being "committed to others" as a factor in their decision-making. For example, Kayla, 39, referred to having children as "demanding" and said her and her husband "can't even commit to a pet". Similarly, Theresa, 39, said "I don't want to meet anybody's emotional needs" and "I want to do whatever I want to do". Likewise, Brandy, 33, said, "I don't want to be responsible for any children". She said she "can't imagine having a mouth to feed and take care of, you know. Nope", and that she likes "not having attachments".

Expense of Raising Children

Six participants reported the financial responsibility of having children as a deterrent in their decision. Phoebe, aged 27, said, "I can hardly afford myself, I can't afford a whole other person. I don't even have a pet". Wendy, 40, explained, "I have to economically support myself… It's like giving my life just to have a baby…, I still have to support my life, myself". Theresa, 39, said seeing her mother "scrape" to provide for her and her siblings was a factor in her decision and not wanting to be in that position. She added,

I also see like, the factors, like, the grid, and the research shows how much money it costs to raise a child from, like, 0 to 18, and then college, and then, and then the kids, like, hate you. So to me, it's just not worth it.

Abigail, 33, mentioned seeing her family members with children in economic distress played a role in her decision. Similarly, Aria, 35, said, "just seeing my friends get married and having their kids, and then seeing pretty much that they're miserable because they have no money". Brandy, 33, said "money and stability and security also played a huge role". She explained that coming from "an impoverished background", she saw several people in her environment who have children "sort of sink deeper into poverty, and their situations became more and more desperate". She said "those children were not necessarily wanted or taken very good care of." She remembered thinking,

Wow, I don't even want kids and I'm looking at this situation and being like, 'What have you done to these poor children? Why are you doing this to them?'

Doubts About Bringing Children Into a Dangerous World

Four participants reported not wanting to bring a child into this world because it is a "scary" place. For example, Wendy, 40, referred to the world as a scary place as she explained that when her older brother, in Indonesia, wanted to send his eldest child to live with her, she discouraged him because she is rarely home. She said this would cause her be in a constant state of worry "because we don't know who his friend will be and I live in the suburb. It's so many drug addicts. The neighbor I cannot trust". Theresa, 39, said, "this world is not an easy place to be, so I feel like I'm sparing a potential, like, soul from having to get chewed up. I couldn't". Likewise, Carol, 27, said "the world is not such a good, pretty place to be in". Aria, 35, said,

I know people always say this, but, like, the world is a scary place. Like, I'm not sure I want to bring a life into this world the way it is right now. I mean, there's so much violence, there's so much discrimination, negativity. I'm just not, I just, right now, I don't think it's the right time either.

Health Reasons

Five participants expressed not wanting to pass on genetic vulnerabilities as a factor in their decision not to have children. Phoebe, 27, worried about passing on "healthcare issues" to a child. She said, "I have a lot of mental and physical illness and that will just be like a terrible trait to pass on". Similarly, Abigail, 33, said her family and her fiancé's family "are both extremely medically complicated families, ranging from clinical issues, cancers, heart conditions, depressions, mental illness, to bi-polar disorder". She said, "I don't know that we need to procreate and put more of our genetics back in the gene pool". She added, "both of us have very significant family histories for substance abuse and everything so I just have never seen the need to reproduce my own genetics". Theresa, 39, said, "alcoholism runs in my family, mental illness runs in my family". She said, "I really think if I have children, that generation is going to, like, suffer". She referenced her religious faith and said, "the Bible says 'the sins of the father will be visited on the third and the fourth generations…, I'm the second generation". She said, "I've been less thrilled with the idea of continuing this genetic, like, when I was in therapy, I once called it I don't want to have a sludge behavior". Carol, 27, said, "I'm pretty sure there is, like, mental health issues…, definitely anxiety issues in my family". She added, "I think there's some kind of, like, genetic thing going on, so I definitely don't want to like, kind of pass that on". Likewise, Erin, 26, said,

> I have a lot of medical problems that I wouldn't want to pass on to somebody. I have a couple of auto-immune issues and I would never want to risk passing it to someone. Like, knowing that I have them, I don't, I wouldn't want to, you know, possibly have to pass that on. It's just, I don't think it's something that would make me happy. I think it would make me actually very unhappy if I did.

Physical Demands of Pregnancy and Childbirth

Four participants reported a "difficult" pregnancy or the pain of childbirth as factors in their decision. Phoebe, 27, made reference to the process of labor. She said, "I know what childbirth does to a person's body, I don't want it, basically". Similarly, Aria, 35, said, "the physical pain of childbirth, I don't really want to go through that". Aria, also talked about seeing her friends' negative experiences of having children and the physical pain of childbirth. She said,

> What made it easier for me to decide is, like, seeing my friends struggle, and knowing that I'd have the same thing. And like, also the physical pain of childbirth, I don't really want to go through that either.

Likewise, Abigail, 33, referred to childbirth, she said, "that's something I would never look forward to". She added,

> That's not me. It's just not something I would feel excited about… I feel like I would be a total mess through my entire pregnancy… I'm convinced that my pregnancy would be the worst pregnancy ever. Of course, that's probably false, but… the possibility of that. I'm just like, no, that's not something I have to endure.

Theresa, 39, said she recently started to detach from her "dependent" mother, and "the idea of having another baby, sucking, literally and figuratively sucking at you is just like, it makes me cringe".

Experience of Being without Children

This section will present data on participants' experiences of being without children. Participants' feelings about being without children were diverse. Responses received from others about their choice were diverse and ranged from positive to negative. The following paragraphs will discuss perceived advantages as well as challenges of being without children.

Perceived Advantages or Benefits of not Having Children

Four participants expressed being "glad", "happy", "thankful", and having a "good relationship" with their partner. For example, when asked whether or not children were part of her life in any way, Carol, 27, said no and added, "I'm kind of glad about that, yes. Yeah, I don't feel like I'm missing out all that much". Similarly, Theresa, 39, said her experience without children has been "fine" and "great". She expressed being "thankful" that when she gets home after a long workday, she does not "have to talk to anyone". She said when she is on Facebook, she sees her old classmates from high school and college with their family and she thinks "I'm so glad I don't have that" because she does not have to "go home and think about cooking for someone" who may not appreciate it. She added, "I don't need that. I'm so happy". Erin, 26, said, "I hate to say it but it's been kind of great". Abigail, 33, reported that her experience of not having children is that her "relationship is good" and that her and her fiancé enjoy spending time with each other. She said, "we do a lot of road trips. We do a lot of things that we didn't get to do as children, or that [her fiancé] didn't get to do as a child, and we get to strengthen our relationship together".

Freedom. All 10 participants talked about having the freedom to do what they please with their time, their money, to travel, and having the opportunity to further their education or advance their careers. For example, Wendy, 40, said she has more free time and is more flexible. She added that she can visit her mother in her native country more often since she has no child whose school she has to worry about or be "present" for. Phoebe, 27, said while she does not receive certain benefits or aids that women with children get, she is able to do what she wants. She further, stated, "I don't have to account for, like, some other life to consider and raise and consider the psychological well-being and all that". Echoing Phoebe's experience, Erin, 26, said she has the freedom to do what she wants. She added, "I can pick up and go on vacation for a month" or "move abroad for a year after graduation and not have to worry about it and sort of the consequences of that". She said, "I like having these opportunities available to me". Erin said being without children has "allowed [her] to go where [she] want[s]educationally". Brandy, 33, said her experience has been "freeing" and that "anything is possible, really, anything is possible". She expressed not having "to put a big weight" on her life that "stops any momentum" she has "as a professional or a personal growth, or theatrical growth". Aria, 35, also said she likes the freedom to "just get up and do whatever" she wants. She added, "I can get up in the middle of the night and go to Walmart and go shopping and not worry about who's going to watch my kid". She described her experience as "freeing". In terms of work, Aria said, "I can have a job where I work nights... and not have to worry about who's going to watch my child because my husband works days".

Financial advantages. Six participants talked about financial relief. For instance, Erin, 26, said she likes having the financial freedom to do what she wants and said, "All my money is my money. I don't have to sort of spend it on other people". She worried about sounding "selfish" but she likes having the freedom to do what she wants to do and when she wants to do it. Brandy, 33, said she is more financially stable and does not have to plan her life around children the way she sees people who have children do. Carol, 27, said it "frees me up a lot in financial responsibility because I only have myself to, like, take care of". Similarly, Theresa, 39, said, "I have a bank account that I can do whatever I want with". She added that having watched her mother "scrape to provide" for her and her siblings, being without children, she does not have to "scrape", which is a "relief".

Challenges of not Having Children

Several participants talked about challenges of not having children. Some reported feeling alienated from friends who are parents, feeling pressured by others, and feeling judged. Lastly, some talked about assumptions that others make about their choice to not have children.

Disconnect from friends/others who are parents. Three participants reported feeling somewhat detached from their friends with children. For instance, Wendy, 40, said, "it's, like, make me like I'm not their best friend anymore because we not going to the park together, we not going to the zoo together" despite having more leisure time than their other friends with children. She added, "sometimes when they talk about something I'm not connected…, and then even my own sister she not talk to me". Similarly, Abigail, 33, referred to her loss of friendships because her friends with children either don't have time anymore or they do but feel as though she would not want to spend time with them. She said that they no longer initiate spending time with her but "they will invite the other mommies over". Abigail shared that a good friend of hers since elementary school has children, who was supposed to be in her upcoming wedding, once told her "'I'm a mom and you're not and I think we're in different places in our lives because of that, and I don't know how to relate to you'". She reported having several similar situations with "multiple friends, family members, and co-workers, who, just for whatever reason feel as though [she] should be having kids".

Hayley, 32, expressed feeling somewhat worried about her relationship with her partner more recently because her friends are having children now. She said, "we don't see them as often, and they don't come out and go out for dinner at 9pm anymore, you, know, they just can't do that anymore". Hayley explained that this has made her partner think about their future, in terms of what they will do with their free time or "what [their] lives would look like". She said this makes him wonder whether or not they should have children.

Pressure from others. Seven participants reported getting pressure from others to have children. For instance, Hayley, 32, recalled being told by friends, "'Why wouldn't you? That's what we did, so why wouldn't you do that?'" She explained that her mother wants grandchildren and does not "respect" her decision. She added, "it comes up in conversation somehow, and not even necessarily asking when I'm going to have, but she'll just have little comments like all my friends have grandchildren now". Kayla, 39, expressed receiving similar "pressure" from her mother and responses from others about her choice. She said the most uncomfortable experience for her was expressing her decision to her parents. She shared that her mother was "very disappointed and upset" and makes her feel uncomfortable about her decision by bringing it up occasionally. Wendy, 40, reported receiving the same "pressure" from her mother. She said before her late partner passed away three years ago, her mother was the one "pushing hard" for her to have children. After she had the miscarriage and her partner passed, she was "relieved" that she did not have the baby.

Feeling judged by others. Eight participants reported feeling judged by others about their choice. For instance, Kayla, 39, talked being called "selfish" by a co-worker.

She made reference to dominant discourse and said, "the burden is on the woman in the sense that it's up, I should be the one that wants this" because her husband is the breadwinner and works long hours; as such, she said, "I should be the one to want it and it's hard to say I don't". She worried that her parents-in-law will "think differently" of her. She added, "it would be easier if I said I couldn't have kids, not that I didn't want to". Wendy, 40, expressed knowing that her mother and her older brother are disappointed in her decision not to have children. She also reported feeling "encouraged" by her doctor to have a baby. She said the doctor asked her at what age her mother reached menopause and told her she still had time and that "It's a beautiful thing to do'". Abigail, 33, reported that her experience with family and friends is that "there's an expectation placed on [her] to have them, and [she doesn't], so there's constant conflict there". She expressed it being "a slight annoyance" when people tell her that she will have children. She said, just recently, her brother-in-law asked, "'So, when you start thinking about having kids? I mean, when are you having kids, and I know you're going to say you're not having them'" and gives her "advice" about it. Other than being asked, Abigail reported being told by her religious and spiritual co-workers and people who don't really know her, "'That's very selfish of you. You know, it's your job, to procreate, and you know, we're put on this earth as women with the gift to bear children and we should do that'", and that it's "irresponsible" of her. Others told her she "should have had children" because she's great with children. They commented that she would make a "great mom". Abigail also referred to people who "unintentionally" judge her and say, "'Oh my gosh, you got to be kidding me, you'd be a great mom'". She also recalled her grandmother's last words to her before she died, "'Make sure you have children or you're going to be alone when you're my age'". As a result of these statements made by others, Abigail noted feeling "a lot of anxiety" and wonders occasionally whether or not she will "regret" her decision in the future. "Thankfully", she said, "I always go back to no, no".

Aria, 35, reported that the "most negative response" she has received was that she is "selfish" by a woman whom she considered her friend, her wedding planner. She recalled feeling "judged". She added,

> I don't think other women really like it very much, but it's not other women's choice, it's my choice, and I don't really care what other women think of me. This is my life, and they're entitled to their opinion, but at the end of the day, I'd be the one taking care of that child, not them.

Aria said that the other responses she has received were "passive-aggressive", such as "'well, you don't have kids, you can do what you want, so you're free from that, good for you'".

Erin, 26, reported that despite having told her mother "multiple times and on several occasions" that she will not have children, her mother and others continue to tell her that she will change her mind when she meets the right person. Erin said "it's just hard for them to understand that decision for me". She added,

> I find it very frustrating when my family gives me a hard time and that, that weirdly enough makes my decision stronger and I'm just, I'm like more not willing to change, I guess… I'm just, like, nope, I'm not gonna listen to that. Like, it's my choice, this is what I'm planning to do.

Referring to dominant discourse, Erin said, "I feel like society as a whole still expects that young women are gonna want kids". She added, "I think there's still that expectation that you know, like, the biological clock is ticking and we should want to, you know, like, fulfill that destiny." Phoebe, 27, said because she made her decision at a young age, "people were surprised" more so about the fact that she reached her decision at such a young age more so than not wanting to have children. She added that occasionally, she is asked why she does not have kids, or whether she has kids and when she says 'no', she does not "listen to what they say after" because it's her decision and that she "demands respect when it comes to stuff like that". She added, "People are just so surprised that a person with a vagina doesn't want to use it". While Phoebe reported people saying, "good, that's responsible of you", she stated, that other people tell her, 'You're gonna get old', to which she responds "'I don't care'". Phoebe also expressed her frustrations with the dominant discourse. She said she has heard of women without children being called "childhaters" and thinks it's "absolutely terrible because we all contribute to making children". She added,

> Why is it that when someone with a penis doesn't want kids that's acceptable but somebody that is expected to give birth to children doesn't want kids, it's like…, oh, we're monsters because we don't want to have kids. This is double standards misogynistic bullshit. I don't fit into the mold.

In contrast to the other participants who reported others' reactions about their decision to not have children, two participants said that was not their experience. Theresa, 39, said people have not responded to her as much as she "thought they would". Interestingly, she said, "I think I have a lot of imaginary dialogues with people that I imagine will question me but they don't". She expressed asking herself whether or not people actually ask her. She said that she might be "on the defensive" and referred back to the 12-step exercise she did about "the lies that people tell themselves" and her expectation that people would require an answer from her.

Carol, 27, said because she is "very guarded" and has an "anticipatory aversion" to being told what she should be doing, she is "reticent" to share her feelings about families with others. However, like Theresa, Carol expressed having built an "imaginary

scenario" in her mind that if she tells them she "would never have kids", they would say,

"'You are too young to decide or you're selfish to decide that". On the other hand, she

reported that the people she has chosen to tell know who she is and know how she would

react if they were unsupportive, so they've just "acquiesced".

 Assumptions made about their choice. All ten participants talked about others'

reactions and assumptions that they will later want to have children. Hayley, 32, stated

that her mother thinks she will have children after her post-doctoral internship next year

when she gets "bored". She also explained that her friends who have children often ask

her when she is going to have a baby and when she says "never", although some people

respect that, others say "'No, no, you will. You will. Of course you will'". Hayley

expressed that she thinks "a lot of people don't understand that it actually is a decision"

that her and her partner have made about their lives. Interestingly, Hayley stated

receiving these comments more often when she was in her 20s, especially when she was

25 years old. People would tell her she was "so young", that she did not know yet what

the future held for her, and that she would change her mind. Now that she is in her 30s,

Hayley said people are starting to believe that she is "biologically, running out of time".

Hayley said she receives a lot of "backlash" for saying she does not want to have

children. She finds it "really frustrating" because she feels she is not taken seriously "at

32 years old to make [her] own decisions about [her] own life". She said each time

people say to her, "'Uh, no, no, it will happen, you'll just do it'".   Brandy, 33, said that

others, especially older women, have told her , "'Oh, just wait'", which she finds

"insulting" because she is 33 years old and people do not believe that she knows "[her] own mind and [her] own body". Brandy also talked about people who wonder whether she has tried to have children but could not. She said though they do not say it directly, they say, "'Oh, you don't have children, oh, oh, okay'" and she has to reassure them that she intentionally does not have them. She explained that these situations at times render her to feel as though she is

> Left out of knowing something,…, like I'm not part of an easily identifiable group or even that there are social experiences that I'm not gonna have because I'm not doing those things. And then people sort of relegate you to this other category of like, awkward, weird.

Lastly, Brandy added that people assume that because she is not married that her boyfriend is a "jerk", a "player", or he does not want to "settle down". She said, "almost like my decision is attached to the fact that we're not married and that somehow he's in the position of power to make that decision". Brandy said, "that gets hard, it gets hard". Carol, 27, reported that some friends have said, "'Well, you say that now, but who knows'" and "'What if you change your mind?'" when she told them she wants to have a "hysterectomy as a preventative medicine".

Although most participants reported feeling "pressure" from family and receiving negative comments about their decision to not have children, several participants stated also receiving some support. Five participants said they felt supported by some family members and friends. For example, Theresa, 39, said she has an aunt who is "childfree" with whom she has discussed her decision and who supports her decision. Two participants reported that their father supports their decision and told them they should do what they want and what makes them happy. One of them, Brandy, 33, said her father disclosed to her as an adult, that he did not want to have children but because her mother wanted to, he went along with it. She said when she told her father about her decision, he said, "'Good, because there's no undoing that'". Brandy also feels "immensely supported "by her friends, some of which also do not have children. As for her friends who do have children, she said some "still get it". Carol, 27, said, in regards to people who really understand her decision, "I can only count them in just with my 5 fingers", because they know what it was like for her growing up. Similarly, Erin, 26, said she tends to gravitate towards people who do not have children; as such, her closest friends are supportive of her decision. Still, she said there are other people who support her decision. She explained that one of her best friends from college who married and had a child at a really young age "backs me up too". She stated, "It's nice to be able to see the people that have the same viewpoint as me". Likewise, Abigail, 33, said some of her former customers with and without children, whom she is still friends with from when she worked as a waitress are "incredibly accepting" of her decision.

Impact on Sense of Self

This section will present data on the impact that participants' decision to not have children had on their sense of self. The participants' responses varied and ranged from no impact to questioning themselves or their choice. Three participants reported that their decision did not affect the way they see or feel about themselves. Two reported a positive impact. For example, Theresa, 39, said she feels good about her decision because she is "sparing a potential victim", and that helps her maintain a sense of authenticity as she is not counting on a baby for self-fulfillment. Brandy, 33, stated she used to feel "selfish" for not wanting to have children but now, she said, "my best is yet to come".

The remaining five participants reported questioning themselves or their choice despite being sure about their decision. For instance, Hayley, 33, said, "sometimes I do feel like, you know, like, why don't I want children?" She questioned if there is "something, like, weird about [me] or weird about not wanting to be a mom". She wondered whether or not she is "missing a gene" because most women "desperately want to have children". She added that she grew up with a very loving mother and grandmother and thinks that her mother "feels like she did something to turn [me] off". Similarly, Kayla, 39, said, "I do think about this, you know, what is it about me that doesn't have that maternal instinct?" She added,

> I don't know if it's just my makeup and it wasn't in the cards for me, I just don't know where it came from, I just know it's been there.

Wendy, 40, wondered, "I don't know, I feel like, do I really weird?" She added, "to have children is a choice, right? So I feel, still, like, I'm still normal". Erin, 26, said due to "family and societal pressures", she thinks of herself as "selfish" sometimes and feels as though she "should want this". As such, Erin stated she does not have the best "view of [her]self". However, she also said being without children has given her confidence. Abigail, 33, reported that her decision has "created a little bit of turbulence" in her life. She said though she feels "anxious" about her decision and has "doubts" about it, she is "very confident" in herself and her choice.

While most participants reported feeling comfortable with their choice, they noted also experiencing some ambivalence and confusion. Participants talked about feeling confused and doubted themselves, and how or why their choice originated. They wondered whether or not they were "abnormal", "missing a gene", or were cynical.

Their accounts suggest that the choice to not have children is not simple and can be emotionally-laden.

Thoughts about the Future

This section will present data on participants' reflections about the way they may feel about the future in regards to their decision to not have children. Some participants' responses reflected concern about who will take care of them in their old age, others did not have any concerns and felt "good" about their decision, still, one participant reported not thinking about it. For example, Phoebe, 27, said though she doubts she will change her mind in the future, if she did, she could adopt a child, which she said she probably would not, but for now, she is not concerned about it because she has "plenty of time to think about it". Three participants reported worrying about who will take care of them when they retire; however, they did not think it was "a good reason to have children". Of these participants, one said maybe she "won't retire". Another one said hopefully the children she is helping support will help take care of her and her husband. For example, Abigail, 33, said, "my number one concern is just making sure that myself and my fiancé are cared for when we're older". She added,

> What if I don't have the money to pay for my own care? When I'm older, who's going to take care of me? My answer to that is all of these wonderful children that I'm paying for their college, right now. They better be there for me. My sister is raising them well to do that.

Carol, 27, worried that she would change her mind in her 30s based on her conversations with other women who said that they did not want to have children in their 20s but later changed their mind in their 30s. She said,

> I talked to like, women in their 30s, and I feel like my fear is my hormone might betray me later on. I mean, they always say that it doesn't matter what you feel in your 20s, in your 30s, you just go haywire and you want to have kids no matter

what. So, that's kind of where I am at this point. But at the point that I really hope that I don't have kids.

Other participants said they would use the money they have saved to support themselves or go to a nursing home. The remaining six participants reported they will not change their mind or will help take care of others, and feeling "good" about their decision. Of these participants, one said she and her husband realize there is a possibility they may regret their decision later but for now, she is without regret, and doubts that she will regret it in the future. For instance, Kayla, 39, said,

> I think we both know that it is not without regret. To what extent when it might actually, really, you know, if and when I should say actually, may hit or something, I don't know. …. So, you know, I am not in the regret phase right now. I'm just not. I don't think I well get to that point because I don't think that at 39 something is suddenly going to shift tremendously in me.

Even though most participants who were in a romantic relationship mentioned being on birth control, three reported that they would "deal with it" if they became pregnant. Theresa, 39, although single and reported not pursuing any romantic relationships, said it goes against her beliefs as a Christian to "end life that's already started." She went on to say that she would rather not get pregnant but said, "if I got pregnant, I would not get an abortion," and added, "if I can stop it before it gets started, I would rally and I would do the best I could to be the best mom I could." Abigail, 33, who mentioned being on birth control, said she "would deal with it" if she became pregnant for fear that her decision would negatively impact her relationship. She said, "I really don't want kids but you know…, if something were to happen, we would deal with it but we're planning on that not happening." She also said,

> The only thing I think could change my decision is, I'm on birth control now, with my fiancé, we're getting married. If somehow I were to get pregnant now, that would be a harder decision because I know that this is the person who I'm

spending my life with … and I would worry about how that type of decision would impact our relationship because my fiancé is okay with it. But if I were to get pregnant, I don't know if he'd be okay with me terminating the pregnancy, so I'd have to do a whole soul-search and evaluation of my whole life to make that decision but we are very protective of that knowing that this is the choice that we made so that'd probably be the only thing that would really rock my world in terms of decision making.

Summary and Conclusion

Participants shared their reflections and experiences of choosing not to have children. Their decision-process, the factors leading to their decision, and the effect on their sense of self were also explored. Lastly, participants reflected on how they may feel about their decision in the future. Their accounts were captivating and compelling. Interviews showed that for many participants, their choice was not necessarily a process but rather, something they "intuitively knew" that solidified later on. While some participants had difficulty recalling when or how they arrived at their decision, several had an idea of or knew what factors played a role in their decision-making. Though their experiences varied, they were similar in many ways. When they recounted their experiences, reasons were an amalgam of: family trauma, growing up with several other children, babysitting, their mother's identification with being a "mom", seeing others with children struggle, limited career opportunities, incompatibility of having a successful career and having children, doubts about their ability to parent, not wanting to meet demands of parenting, the world being a dangerous place, freedom, financial reasons, health reasons, and pregnancy and pain of childbirth.

In regards to their experience of being without children, the interviews revealed that there were both advantages and disadvantages to their choice. The perceived advantages were related to having the freedom to do what they want, when they want to and having financial stability/freedom. Some participants felt "free" and "independent".

The challenges discussed were related to loss of friendships, receiving unsolicited advice

or getting pressure from others with or without children, and feeling judged. Some also

talked about others' assumptions about their choice. The majority of the participants

reported that others with or without children assumed they would change their mind.

Interestingly, one participant talked about people assuming that the choice was her

partner's and thought her partner was irresponsible or stringing her along. As for the

impact their decision had on their sense of selves, the majority of participants reported

getting "pressure" from family, friends, co-workers, and sometimes strangers. These

"pressures" at times triggered a sense of ambivalence about their choice or rendered the

participants to question themselves. One participant was so worried about changing her

mind in the future that she said she would like to have a hysterectomy. Despite these

"pressures", most participants stated feeling "great" or gaining a strong "self-esteem" and

"confidence" resulting from their decision. One participant reported that she has more

time to work on her relationship with her fiancé. In terms of participants' thoughts about

the future, interviews showed that though the majority of the participants worried about

who would take care of them in their old age, they felt it was not a good reason to have

children. This finding shows that the choice to not have children is complex and that

several factors can impact one's decision, including others' opinions (See table 3). The

results and findings will be discussed in more detail in Chapter Five.

Table 3. Quick Reference Data About the Findings

Major Themes	Minor Themes	N
Decision-Process	Not remembering making a decision	N= 9
	Decision made since childhood	N= 2
	Decision made in teenage years	N= 7
	Vacillating about decision	N= 6
	Difficulty of decision:	
	Pressure from mother	N= 7
	Ease of decision:	
	Knowing & friend support	N= 6
	Soul-searching/Self-evaluation	N= 4
	Romantic relationship:	
	Did not/would not impact choice	N= 8
	Check-ins	N= 5
Factors Leading to Choice	Background experiences:	
	Family abuse	N= 2
	Growing up with other children	N= 3
	Mother's identification	N= 3
	Doubts about ability to parent	N= 8
	Impact on career/education	N= 7
	Not Wanting to meet others' demands	N= 7
	Expense of raising children	N= 6
	Dangerous world	N= 4
	Health reasons	N= 5
	Physical demands of pregnancy & labor	N= 4
Experience of Being Without Children	Perceived advantages:	
	Freedom	N= 10
	Financial freedom/stability	N= 6
	Challenges:	
	Alienation from friends & others	N= 3
	Pressure from others	N= 7
	Being judged	N= 8
	Dealing with others' assumptions	N= 10
Impact on Sense of Self	No impact	N= 3
	Positive impact	N= 2
	Question self/Choice	N= 5
Thoughts About the Future	Worried about care in old age	N= 3
	Not Worried/ will prepare for that	N= 6
	Worried will change mind later on	N= 1
	Would deal with pregnancy	N= 3

CHAPTER FIVE

DISCUSSION

The intent of this chapter is to discuss and interpret the results presented in Chapter Four. In this chapter, the findings from the participants' narratives that were most significant will be presented and examined to elucidate the women's overall subjective experiences of being without children. The following sections will provide a review of the study, a discussion of the results, strengths and areas of limitations of the study, the implications for clinical practice, recommendations for future research, and the conclusions obtained from the study.

Review of the Study

The purpose of this study was to explore the intentional choice of ten adult women who have decided not to have children. Previous studies have looked at the experiences of women who have made that choice; however, the experience of women born after the second wave of the feminist movement who made this decision has not received as much research attention. A semi-structured interview approach was used to guide the study as well as encourage the women to reflect on their overall experiences. This approach permitted the women to openly explore and discuss their personal experiences as well as allowed the researcher to gain a more in-depth insight into aspects of this experience that were relevant to the participants. Questions were asked about how the women arrived at their choice, what factors, if any, played a role in their decision, and what the decision process was like, including what they felt made their choice more difficult or easy. The participants were asked to reflect on their experience of being without children and whether or not their choice had an impact on their sense of self.

105

They were also asked about how others in their lives responded to their choice and what the impact of this was for them. Lastly, the participants were asked to discuss how they anticipate they may feel about their choice in the future. Questions sought to elicit information that would enable the researcher to better understand their choice.

Interpretation of Findings

A more recent study by Livingston and Cohn (2010) showed that approximately one in five American women choose not to bear children, whereas, in the 1970s, one in ten women was without children. It is noteworthy that although this study included only ten women, several months after the interviews were conducted, more than triple the number of women who participated in this study continued to call in order to participate. The reason explained was that they felt compelled to have their story heard, and some expressed gratitude for such a study.

The complexity of the decision to choose to be without children has been discussed in the literature (DeLyser, 2011; Gillespie, 2003; McQuillan, Greil, Shreffler, Wonch-Hill, Gentzler, & Hathcoat, 2012) and was echoed in this study. Also of similarity were the myriad and complex factors affecting their choice as well as their subjective experiences (Doyle, Pooley, & Breen, 2015; Gold, 2012; Kroll, 2011; Park, 2005).

Major and Minor Themes

This section will discuss some of the key themes identified in the analysis of the participants' interview material. These themes relate to the decision-process, factors impacting the choice to be without children, the experience of not having children, whether or not the choice had an impact on the participants' sense of self, and their thoughts about the future. Major themes are defined as topics that were endorsed by five or more participants, whereas minor themes refer to themes that were indicated by less than five women.

As reflected in the literature (Houseknecht, 1979), all women who participated in the study were early articulators, defined as women who made the choice to be without children early in life, particularly before meeting their significant others. In terms of the decision-process, a common theme identified was that women reported that they did not specifically remember making a deliberate decision about not having children. Many reported knowing that they did not want to have children since they were teenagers; some reported being very sure of this decision when they were children. This is consistent with the findings in the literature (Park, 2005; Peterson and Engwall, 2013), as the majority of the participants talked about not remembering making a decision, but rather expressed that it was something they "always knew" that solidified in their teenage years.

Approximately two thirds of the participants expressed feeling pressured from their mothers to have children. This may demonstrate that the decision to move away from traditional family life is difficult. Some participants indicated that their mother's desire to be grandmothers made them question their choice and made it difficult to feel settled in their choice. They indicated that they were often told that their decision made their mothers sad, disappointed, or upset. Some reported that being asked when they would have children despite having mentioned several times that they would not was intolerable. Other participants added that they felt frustrated having the same conversation, and especially being told that they would change their mind. One participant mentioned that she felt "insulted", as though she could not make her own decision or know what she desires. Another participant reported feeling frustrated when her mother asked her who would take care of her in her old age, to which she stated that she hoped her mother did not have her "thinking that that was sort of the end result." Looking back at the age of the participants who endorsed feeling pressure from their mothers, it ranged from 26 to 40 years old, suggesting that despite the social advances resulting from the feminist movement, some mothers may continue to see being a mother as an accomplishment that would render their daughters fulfilled or happy. Further, the women who did not report feeling pressured from their mothers did not deny being pressured, but rather, they did not feel that the pressure affected their sense of self or choice.

Although the majority of the participants reported that this had been a decision made when they were younger, this decision was not made without vacillation. For instance, some participants discussed evaluating themselves and questioning whether or not there was something inherently wrong with them, since most women in their environment talked about wanting to become mothers. One woman talked about vacillating on her decision because all her friends were getting married and having children, and she felt "stressed" about going on a different path. Another participant worried about what she would do with the free time not having children would afford her. Others said they wondered what it would be like to be mothers, but simply did not feel it was the right decision for them. It is worth mentioning that the majority of the participants reported feeling more confident in their choice once they felt validated either by a friend, family member, or learning about other women who made the same choice. This suggests that despite knowing they did not want to have children, knowing that other women feel as they do normalized their experience and made it easier to make a final decision.

Of interest was the impact of friends and romantic partners on this process. As indicated above, the majority of participants reported that receiving the support of friends helped make the decision easier. They expressed that being in a romantic relationship did not or would not impact their choice. All women who were either married or in a romantic relationship revealed that they occasionally "checked in" with their partner. One participant worried that her fiancé would change his mind in the future and resent her for not wanting to have children, as he has occasionally vacillated on the topic of whether or not to have children. She expressed being concerned that if her fiancé ever decided to have children, that it might be "too late for [her] then." Others worried that they would get in the way of their partners from experiencing fatherhood and were adamant about not causing their partners "to suffer". Some participants were concerned about the relationship dissipating as they indicated that having children would be a "deal-breaker" should their partner change their mind. While the women expressed feeling confident in their decision, it appeared that being in a romantic relationship made the choice somewhat more difficult as they also accounted for their partner's feelings. This supports the notion that making the choice to forego motherhood is not simple, particularly when in a romantic relationship. This revelation reflects the shift indicated in the literature (Mueller and Yoder, 1999; Park, 2005) that women have begun to feel comfortable making that choice. This difference may explain more acceptance from society or perhaps feelings of empowerment on the part of the women despite society's expectations. Given six participants discussed vacillating on their decision, and eight stated being in a romantic relationship has not or would not impact their choice, it is wondered whether the latter is more likely. Alternatively, it may be a combination of both societal acceptance and women empowerment.

It is also worth noting that the majority of the women in this study discussed having some sort of relationship with children. All ten participants reported having children in their lives, either through family, friends, or work. Other than one participant who reported not really liking children, all nine others reported thinking positively about children. They referred to children as "adorable", "cute", and entertaining, and reported enjoying spending time with them, as long as it was not permanent. Three participants reported that their love for children as a major reason they would rather not procreate. As previously discussed, these women were concerned of the environment's negative influence on children, such as racism, the world being a "tough place", and not wanting them to suffer. One participant discussed not wanting to have children because she would want to dedicate her life to her children, which would not be adaptable. Others stated they would rather adopt instead of contributing to the world's overpopulation, given so many children around the world need a safe and loving environment. This is an important finding as in the past, previous research has failed to mention that women who have chosen not to have children have decided to do so despite having some sort of connection to them. This failure to mention it may have contributed to the thought that women who do not want to have children are "childhaters". Similarly, that these women's decision does not reflect a lack of exposure to or appreciation of children, but rather, a conscious choice, and that enjoying children's company is not mutually exclusive to wanting to have children.

The minor themes in the decision-process were: the choice emanating from "soul-searching" or "self-evaluation", endorsed by four women. The participants who reported knowing since childhood were adamant about their choice and made it clear that it did not matter to them what others believed. One of these four women indicated having experienced trauma directly and vicariously, the remaining three did not report having experienced any adverse experience, but rather grew up in or worked in an environment where they saw parents "struggle" financially. One participant reported growing up with several children in her household discouraged her from having children, one mentioned her mother's strong identification of being a mother being something she did not relate to nor looked forward to. Others discussed the world being a dangerous place, and lastly, some indicated not wanting to go through the rigors of pregnancy and childbirth. While this finding was endorsed by a minority of the participants, it was consistent with early decision making, and may provide a context for understanding how these women came to such an early decision. Those who indicated that they evaluated themselves were more likely to have vacillated on their decision due to reported pressure from others, especially from their mothers.

In trying to understand some of the reasons why the participants had chosen not to have children, the participants identified a number of key factors that had contributed to their decision. They reported experiencing doubts about their ability to parent, expressing the worry that they did not have what it takes to be a good parent. Participants expressed concern about the financial impact and expense of raising children. Some participants identified concerns about the impact of parenting on their career or education, and not having the desire to fulfill the demands of parenting. Others referred to having children as "demanding" and expressed not wanting to "commit" themselves to others, including pets, and noted that they felt good about "not having any attachments". Others discussed not wanting to meet others' emotional needs, not being responsible for children, and being able to do whatever they desire, without feeling guilty. A number of participants expressed concern about their ability to be fully present for their child. Further, the impact on career and education as a factor suggest that these women want to be in a position to be financially stable but even then, if this impacted the amount of time they could spend with their children, they did not consider it a worthy choice. Lastly, half of the participants discussed their health issues as a factor in that they do not want to pass on genetic vulnerabilities. They explained that mental illness and/or physical illness run in their families, and they did not feel particularly comfortable bringing a child into this world if there was a possibility that the child would inherit those traits. One participant was adamant about her child "suffering" given the medical and psychiatric issues that run in her family, and indicated that in not having children, she is "sparing a victim". These concerns are consistent with Mollen's (2006) finding, as the participants expressed some fear of passing on genetic vulnerabilities. In this study, half of the participants reported they would be "very unhappy" if they passed on their genetic illness to their children. As reflected in the literature review (Gold, 2012), this study supported the finding that women who decide not to have children consider several factors including some related to their lifestyle as well as concerns for the well-being of the child and the environment.

The minor themes discussed were as Housekenecht's 1979 study suggested, family of origin did not appear to have a strong link to the decision to remain without children despite what previous studies reported. Further, in Gold's 2012 study, the participants had a negative view of the physical demands of pregnancy and childbirth. The participants in that study referred to pregnancy as "barbaric" and did not want to put their bodies through such difficulties. Similarly, in this study, some women referred to pregnancy, particularly the process of childbirth as something they would rather not experience. One participant indicated that she "would never look forward to that", and another reported being aware of what pregnancy does to a woman's body and stated that she "basically [doesn't] want it."

Participants did not only discuss the disadvantages they considered to be integral in becoming a mother, they also identified the advantages of not having children. The most endorsed aspects of this was the freedom they felt to come with not having children. As reflected in the literature (Doyle et al., 2015; Gillespie, 2003; Hird & Abshoff, 2000; Park, 2005), freedom was the most cited advantage of not having children. This included freedom of choice related to resources of time and money. The participants in this study described being grateful for the ability to do what they pleased and when they pleased. They recognized the increased freedom and control over their time. This was also recognized as allowing them more freedom to choose an education or a career that they enjoy in lieu of a career path that would be shaped by the need to devote time to be with their children. The participants also recognized increased financial stability as a perceived advantage of not having children. According to a report by Lino, Kuczynski, Rodriguez, and Schap (2015), using a sample of 23,297 married-couple households and 7,030 single-parent households, the estimated expense to raise a child from birth through at least age 17 years is $233,610 in 2015 in a middle-income, married-couple family. The authors indicated that both direct and indirect costs of raising children are considerable, and absorbs a significant share of the overall household budget. This finding is interesting as it echoed the majority of the participants' concerns about not having enough resources to raise children. Furthermore, a Pew Research Center survey and analysis of Census data (2013) that explores views, values, and economic realities of more than 1, 800 mothers and fathers in the workplace, the women were much more likely than fathers to express that taking time off from work to care for their children hurt their career overall. It is also worth noting that while mothers felt taking the time off negatively impacted their career, they reported feeling glad that they took the time off. This finding supports the participants' concerns about gender roles, in that women are usually the ones to have to put their careers on hold.

A minority of the participants identified that being without children contributed to some feelings of alienation from friends. As noted above, half of the participants worried that their friendships with those who have become parents would dissipate. Others reported concern about having more free time to do what they please, however, not having available friends to spend that time with. Others mentioned feeling "different" or "abnormal" because they lacked the desire to become mothers when their friends looked forward to becoming parents. The participants noted that this difference between themselves and their friends led them to question themselves and their choice, wondering whether or not there was "something wrong with [them]". This theme was also reflected in the literature review (DeLyser, 2011; Park, 2005) in which women who talked about vacillating on their decision experienced moments where they questioned their choice due to others' pressures; however, the experience was described as transient. In this study, while some of the women attributed their doubts to external factors, others recognized that they also struggled with internal factors, such as wondering whether or not they were "missing a gene" and waiting for the desire to bestow onto them. These accounts suggest that the decision to forgo motherhood is complex, multi-dimensional, and includes times when the participants experience ambivalence and conflict, as well as concern that over time and context, their decision may change in subtle ways.

In terms of their thoughts about the future, participants discussed their awareness of the role that children play in the lives of parents as parents age. They addressed the issue of who would take care of them in their old age. The women in this study talked about thinking about their future, and felt that the need to have someone care for them in their old age was not sufficient grounds to have children. They recognized the need to prepare for old age. According to DeLyser, 2011's study, the older participants reported not regretting their decision. The participants in this study did not anticipate that they would regret their decision, although they were aware that they may be missing something.

A minority of the participants discussed a benefit of being without children as spending more time with their significant others. One participant reported that she has more time to work on her relationship with her fiancé. Another participant indicated that not having children allows her to have a "good" relationship with her partner. She added that they are able to "strengthen [their] relationship together" because they can now afford to do things that her partner did not have the opportunity to do as a child.

Overall, the experiences of women who reported being in relationships did not significantly differ from those who did not. The single participants in the study were more concerned about finding a partner who feels similarly about not wanting to have children. The remaining participants who reported being in a relationship worried that their partners would change their mind in the future. The main difference was that those who were in a relationship worried about the long-term impact of their decision on the relationship despite having discussed their choice with their partner at the onset of the relationship.

'Unplanned' Children

An unanticipated finding was the degree of concern expressed by participants that they may become pregnant in an unplanned and unintended way. One participant expressed the fear that when she reached her 30s her 'hormones' would 'betray' her and lead her to change her mind. Her fear of this occurring was sufficient to lead her to consider having a hysterectomy. A few participants reported that despite not wanting to have children and using caution to avoid that, if by any chance they became pregnant, they would keep the baby, either because abortion ran counter to their religious beliefs, or for two participants, out of concern that it would negatively impact their romantic relationship. This was surprising because these two women had previously stated that being in a romantic relationship has not or would not impact their decision. These two participants were in committed relationships and discussed that their partners vacillated on the decision. They explained that while their partners were aware of and in agreement with their choice not to have children, at times, their partners wondered what it would be like to have children. This suggests that perhaps the importance of being in a happy relationship superseded their choice. Paradoxically, these same women expressed frustrations about their mothers' advice that once they find their ideal partner, they would change their mind. This intersection hints at society's insidious and strong influence on women's reproductive choice and leaves open the question of whether or not these women's partners also worried about the impact of their own vacillation on the relationship.

Lastly, half of the participants in the study were enrolled in Psychology programs. This is important to note, as the patient-therapist relationship has parallels with the caregiver or parent relationship. Some participants stated enjoying working with children, and providing them support. Given some of the participants referenced their careers as being "draining" and worried that it would get in the way of their ability to be fully present for their own children, it leaves open the question of whether or not they have found other ways through their careers to express the "nurturing" part of themselves.

Strengths and Limitations of Study

Using a qualitative, exploratory approach method is useful in generating questions that directly target the intended study. Further, using a semi-structured approach allows participants to more fully describe their subjective experience by giving them control over the amount of information they share. However, this approach, while is helpful in guiding the study, can also limit participants' answers to only the questions asked. Therefore, the use of this method has its limitations as it can make it difficult to generate full answers and thus, firm conclusions.

Strengths of this study were considered to be the fact that it allowed for a more in-depth understanding of the women's subjective experience. Additionally, it solicited women who specifically chose not to have children regardless of sexual orientation and relationship status. It also looked at women who were born after the second wave of feminism (mid-1960s through 1970s), which was of interest, given this group has been under-researched. Also of importance is that this study solicited women of different races and ethnicities, as well as religious and educational background.

While this study solicited for a more inclusive population, the sample, however, was a limitation. The study only included a total of ten women, of which only one was an African-American woman, and only one was bi-sexual. Further, the majority of the participants had higher education, and was enrolled in a Psychology program. It would have been interesting to have a more diverse group of women as cultural factors may have played a role in their experiences. Lesbian women and women with less than a high school education were not represented in this study, partly due to the fact that the sample represented participants who were interested in having their stories heard as opposed to being randomized. Therefore, the results found cannot be generalized to the population.

It is also worth noting that the researcher, herself, fits the description of the women in the study; therefore, it is possible that despite efforts to guard her biases, some of them entered the study through the use of semi-structured questions or techniques used during the interview, possibly through body language or countenance. The researcher's experience as a woman who has chosen not to have children was the basis for her interest in the study as well as guided the design and methodology. As such, it is possible that her experience ultimately informed the questions and her interpretation of the data.

Recommendations for Future Research

This study, though consistent with the extant literature, included some limitations, as mentioned in the above paragraph. Further, the literature review covered in Chapter two also indicated some limitations in the methodology. This is often due to the difficulty in finding participants willing to talk about their experience, especially when the topic is still considered a stigma. The literature review listed some limitations, such as using a small sample size, a lack of diversity of the participants, including race and ethnicity, education level, and socioeconomic status. Further, some of the studies did not specifically discern between women who were voluntarily without children or not. Lastly, most of the women included in those studied were between the ages of 40 and 44 years. It would be important to understand the experience of women under the age of 40 years, including a more diverse group of women in terms of race, sexual orientation, and education level. It would also be interesting to explore the decision-process of women who are in the process of making the choice in lieu of relying on memories of how they made the choice and what, in retrospect, most significantly impacted their choice. Lastly, because this study only included participants until 40 years of age, it leaves open the question of whether or not older participants would have felt differently about their experience in terms of regret.

Implications for Clinical Practice

Many women who seek therapy often do so as a result of struggling with issues of identity and life choice. These struggles often lead to an insecure sense of self and conflicts about one's identity, which may contribute to various psychological disorders. Included in those disorders are depression, anxiety, or substance use disorders to combat the internal turmoil that some women face. While the women in this study expressed being comfortable with their choice, some indicated feeling negatively about themselves occasionally due to the continued stigmatization (i.e., pressure, assumptions about their choice, being judged, etc.) of the choice to not have children. For women who do not have the support of family and friends and who lack appropriate coping skills to deal with the stress, important clinical implications are raised for therapists working with such clients. Therefore, understanding more about the process of how women make the choice to not have children and how that decision affects their sense of themselves can provide important insights for clinicians working with these women. Also of importance is the idea that young women have an increased awareness of a range of options or choices around lifestyle, including becoming a mother or not. Given society's continued influence on the way women feel about their choice, it is highly important for these women to find a place where their experience can be normalized and validated. Lastly, it would be important for these issues to be addressed on a societal and cultural level so that both men and women could feel more at ease with the decision to not have children. Given some women in this study expressed concerns about the impact of their choice on their relationship, it would be helpful if these issues were addressed more on a global level so as to make the issue less of a women's problem.

Summary and Conclusion

This study provides some preliminary conclusions about the experience of women who voluntarily chose not to have children, including how they arrived at their choice and what factors played a role in their decision. The findings of this study were strikingly similar to the results found in the literature review, despite the age difference. Further, this study suggests that while society continues to view women who make this choice negatively, over the years, it has become more accepted as many of the participants reported feeling supported from friends and family, and no outside pressure. As mentioned in the literature review, several factors impacted the women's choice, including freedom, doubts about their ability to parent, the expense of raising children,

feeling that they have to choose between work and motherhood, impact on career and

education, and health reasons, among others listed above. Although this study cannot be

generalized to the population due to some of the limitations referenced above, the

findings, however, were consistent with the literature. Additionally, it points to further

research in terms of looking at a more diverse group of women, specifically in terms of

race, socioeconomic status, and sexual orientation, designed in this study but not

captured.